Becoming an Independent Security Consultant

Second Edition

Becoming an Independent Security Consultant

Second Edition

A Practical Guide to Starting and Running a Successful Security Consulting Practice

Michael A. Silva, CPP, CSC

2024

This publication is designed to provide accurate and authoritative information in regard to the subject matter covered. It is sold with the understanding that the publisher is not engaged in rendering legal, accounting, or other professional services. If legal advice or other expert assistance is required, the services of a competent professional person should be sought — From a Declaration of Principles jointly adopted by a Committee of the American Bar Association and a Committee of Publishers and Associations.

First Printing: 2024

Silva Consultants
PO Box 8799
Covington, Washington 98042 USA
www.silvaconsultants.com
Telephone: +1 (888) 645-2299
Email: publisher@silvaconsultants.com

ISBN-13: 978-1-7378587-4-4
ISBN-13: 978-1-7378587-5-1 (Ebook)

Table of Contents

Preface

I have been practicing as an independent security consultant for more than 35 years. I operated my own consulting business during most of this time, although I did do a five-year stint working for one of the largest security consulting firms in the world just to see how it was done by the "big boys".

Although I have deliberately kept my security consulting practice small, I consider it to be a success. The work has been very rewarding from both a financial and personal satisfaction perspective. I have performed projects all across the United States and have been blessed to work for some of the largest corporations in the world, as well as for numerous city, county, and state government agencies.

Due to the success of my consulting practice, I regularly get calls or emails from people wanting to become security consultants. Many of these people have military or law enforcement backgrounds or are soon retiring from a security management position. I try to encourage these people, but also gently explain that no matter how valuable their previous experience is, they are still probably a long way from having the skills necessary to become a successful security consultant.

In response to the many inquiries that I received, I wrote the book "*Becoming an Independent Security Consultant - A Practical Guide to Starting and Running a Successful Security Consulting Practice*" in 2016. This book was purchased by many people considering entering the security consulting profession .

After publishing the first edition of this book, I began to get contacted by people who had read my book and were seeking additional advice and encouragement before starting their own consulting practice. I am pleased to say that many of these people went on to start consulting practices using some or all of the techniques in my book. Some of these people have become very successful and now probably earn more money per year than I do. I am extremely happy for them.

Unfortunately, this is not the case for everyone. Many people start their consulting practice and then give up in a year or less. Some of the common reasons given for closing their business include: *"I can't get enough paying work"*, *"my family needs a steady paycheck"*, or *"I like doing consulting, but don't know how to sell my services or how to run a business"*.

My goal in writing this book is to help aspiring consultants to overcome some of the common causes of failure by giving you the benefit of my more than 35 years of experience. Hopefully, this will reduce your learning curve and increase your chances of success as you begin your journey into security consulting.

A lot has changed since 2016 when I wrote the first edition of this book. This new edition continues to provide the foundational information necessary to establish a successful security consulting practice but has been updated to reflect the conditions that have changed since I wrote the first book. I have also incorporated the answers to the many questions that I have received from readers since the first edition was published. Also included are new chapters that expand upon some important subjects and provide new tips on ways that consultants can maximize their potential for success.

It is my sincere hope that in some small way this book will contribute to the emergence of a new generation of professional independent security consultants.

Introduction

This book is intended as a practical guide to starting and running a successful independent security consulting practice. The goal is to provide practical "how-to" advice rather than generalized or theoretical information.

The focus of this book will be on security management consulting and technical security consulting, the two areas in which I have had the most experience. This book will not talk in depth about forensic security consulting or cybersecurity consulting, although practitioners in these areas may benefit greatly from many of the topics in this book.

This book will concentrate primarily on the business and marketing aspects of running a security consulting practice – the two things that most beginning consultants struggle with the most. This book will not teach you the skills of your chosen security specialty – I'm assuming that you already have these skills and now want to apply them as an independent security consultant. If you do need help in learning how to conduct a security assessment, how to write security policies and procedures, or how to improve your other technical skills, there are plenty of other books already written on these topics.

The things that I write about in this book are things that I have actually done – not just things that I have thought about or things that I would like to do. Much of the advice I give is based on personally having done things the wrong way the first time around. If you are looking for a quick and easy way to succeed, some of the things I tell you may not be what you want to hear.

This book is primarily directed to the individual person who wants to operate their own security consulting practice as a sole practitioner without any employees.

The information in this book assumes that the consulting practice will be operated in the United States and provides information from a US perspective. Readers in other parts of the world may have to adapt some of my advice to fit the customs followed in their own particular countries.

Chapter 1 - What is an Independent Security Consultant?

The dictionary defines a consultant as a "person who provides expert advice professionally", "one who consults another", and "one who gives professional advice or services". It would be natural to assume then that a "security consultant" is a person that provides expert security advice professionally.

Unfortunately, within the security industry, the term "security consultant" has been hijacked. The majority of the people who use this title are in fact sellers of security products and services, and while these people probably do "consult" on a limited basis, their primary goal is to sell the particular product or service that they represent.

Some people who provide personal protection or bodyguard services or conduct investigations may also refer to themselves as "security consultants".

To make a distinction between actual security consultants and others who may call themselves that, the term "independent security consultant" was coined. This term is used to describe professionals who provide expert security advice but who are unaffiliated with any other security product or service. Like an accountant, doctor, or attorney, the independent security consultant charges a fee for their services, and derives no revenue from the sale of products that they recommend.

The exact number of independent security consultants in the world is unknown, but the leading organization representing independent consultants, the International Association of Professional Security Consultants (IAPSC), currently has under 150 members. Even if the total number of practicing consultants is three or four times this number, independent security consultants still make up only a tiny fraction of the security industry as a whole.

Security Consulting Is a Niche Business

There are still many members of the public and even people within the security industry that don't understand what an independent security consultant does or what services they provide. As a result, many independent security consultants face an uphill battle when selling their services: they must first make clients aware of their services, sell the client on the benefits of using an independent consultant, and then convince the client that they are the right consultant for the job.

Although the use of independent security consultants has become much more prevalent now than when I first started in 1985, there is still a lack of understanding of the role of the independent security consultant. The vast majority of businesses with security problems don't even think to call in an independent security consultant, and instead call a guard company, security systems installer, locksmith, or police crime prevention officer when they need security advice.

The market for security consulting services is also limited. Most smaller businesses and private homeowners, as much as they may need security consulting services, simply cannot afford to pay for them. Most larger corporations and organizations have well-staffed in-house security departments, minimizing the need for them to hire an outside security consultant.

Because of these factors, security consulting remains a niche business. I estimate that 70% of potential business clients will never see the need for an independent security consultant and will never hire one. This leaves only about 30% of potential clients who understand the benefits of using an independent security consultant, lack the resources to handle their security problems in-house, and can afford to pay for consulting services.

Fortunately for us independent security consultants, this remaining 30% still provides us with ample opportunity to stay busy and make a good living.

Types of Security Consultants

There are four primary categories or types of security consultants:

Security Management Consultants

Security management consultants are the "general practitioners" of the security consulting profession. Security management consultants provide generalized advice on managing a client's overall security and loss prevention program. Security management consultants typically conduct security assessments, write security policies and procedures, provide security training, assist in recruiting and developing security personnel, and help with the procurement of security products and services.

Forensic Security Consultants

Forensic security consultants provide advice and testimony related to litigation and legal matters. Forensic security consultants are typically retained by attorneys to serve as expert witnesses in a court of law or other legal proceeding. Forensic security consultants review evidence, conduct site surveys, perform threat and risk assessments and provide analysis, opinions and testimony concerning specific legal cases.

Technical Security Consultants

Technical security consultants, sometimes called "security engineers", provide advice related to physical and electronic security systems. Technical security consultants design security systems for new and existing buildings, develop specifications for security equipment, assist with the procurement of security systems and provide oversight of the security system installation process.

Cybersecurity Consultants

Cybersecurity consultants, sometimes called "IT security consultants" or "information security consultants", provide advice related to the security of computers, networks, and communications systems. Cybersecurity consultants conduct risk and vulnerability assessments, perform penetration tests, develop security policies and procedures, and design and specify measures to protect the integrity of the client's information technology systems.

Areas of Practice

While some security consultants operate strictly within the boundaries of the categories defined above, it is very common to see overlap between practice areas. For example, many security management consultants also provide forensic security consulting services. Also, it is now common to see technical security consultants developing skills in the area of cybersecurity.

The independent security consultant's area of practice may also evolve over time. When I started my practice back in 1985, I came from a security systems installation and service background and initially launched my practice as a technical security consultant. I soon discovered, however, that my clients were having difficulty in telling me what they wanted in the way of security systems because they had no idea of what their security risks were or how to manage them.

To fill this void, I developed skills as a security management consultant, and soon found that the demand for this aspect of security consulting was equal to the demand for technical security consulting services. I now provide both security management consulting services and technical security consulting services.

Specialties

While most independent security consultants serve a wide variety of different clients in their practice area, some choose to further specialize. For example, some security management consultants specialize in doing just schools, just hospitals or just retail establishments. Some consultants choose to specialize in providing just a specific service, such as workplace violence training or travel security.

Allied Professions

Many other professionals in the security industry also claim to be capable of providing security consulting services. These include private investigators, firms that provide security guard or executive protection services, and installers of security and surveillance systems.

Some of these firms have established "security consulting" divisions that they claim are operated separately from their other businesses, allowing them to be completely objective. In some cases, the consulting services provided by these firms are offered for free or at a reduced cost as a benefit to clients who purchase their other products or services.

The International Association of Professional Security Consultants (IAPSC) has strict policies on who may become a member and currently prohibits private investigators and those who have affiliations with security products or guard companies from becoming members. Some people feel that this is unfair and arbitrarily limits who may become a member, while others feel that the strict independence policy is necessary to maintain the integrity of the organization.

Ultimately, it is up to the client to decide who is qualified to provide them with security consulting services. Some will feel that using a consultant that is completely independent is necessary, while others see no problem at all in using a "consultant" that just happens to sell other security products and services.

Chapter 2 - A Week in the Life of a Security Consultant

Readers of the first edition of this book told me that they particularly enjoyed the chapter "A *Week in the Life of a Security Consultant*". This chapter was written to give the prospective security consultant some idea of what a typical week in the life of a security consultant might look like.

The following is an updated version of this narrative based on one of my recent weeks. This narrative is based on my experience as a consultant who provides both security management consulting and technical security consulting. Security consultants practicing in other areas would likely have a different story to tell.

Monday

7:00 AM: I am contacted by a company doing a study for the US Department of Labor. They request that I complete a survey to establish security-related job descriptions for an occupational information database. I agree and complete an online questionnaire consisting of over 100 questions. I get numerous requests to participate in surveys and focus groups. I feel that this type of unpaid activity is one part of being a professional in this industry and I try to participate as time permits.

8:00 AM: I begin work on a massive security assessment report for a very prominent luxury gated residential community. I review my written notes and audio recordings and begin to create an outline for my report.

11:00 AM: I research the history of published news articles concerning the gated community that I am writing the report for. I am surprised at the number of articles written and learn some interesting new details about the project.

12:00 PM: I get a call from a client that operates paper mills across the United States. I have already done assessments at two of this client's mills and am asked to provide an estimate of what it would cost to do yet another one at a paper mill on the east coast. He is not ready for a proposal at this point, so I give him an approximate cost that he can plug into his budget for the following year.

1:00 PM: I take a break for lunch and check my social media accounts. I attempt to stay active on social media and try to make comments or post new messages at least several times per week.

1:30 PM: I begin to analyze the over 2,000 security incident reports that I have received from my gated community project. I find that the incidents are not well classified, requiring me to read through each and every report to get a picture of what's going on. This tedious work is not something that I particularly enjoy but is something that must be done.

4:30 PM: I receive an email from a contractor with questions about a project that I designed three years ago. I thought that this project was already completed, but apparently the client postponed it, and it is just getting underway now. Because my memory of the project is beginning to fade, I have to review my RFP and drawings in order to properly answer the questions. I have had design projects go on for as long as seven years, so I have found that it is essential to maintain good documentation.

6:00 PM: I am about a third of the way through my review of the incident reports when my wife calls me for dinner. Reading through the incident reports proved to be less boring than I thought. I am amazed at how many non-security activities the security officers at this community are asked to perform.

Tuesday

7:00 AM: I drive into the city to conduct a site inspection at a high-rise condominium that I am designing a video surveillance system upgrade project for. Traffic is heavy and I'm thankful that I have my assistant (who also happens to be my wife) with me so that I can use the carpool lanes.

8:00 AM: We arrive at the condominium, meet briefly with the manager to check out an access card and keys, and then begin exploration of the property on our own. This condominium consists of three large towers and a huge multilevel parking garage. We decide to begin at the lowest level and work our way up.

9:00 AM: We soon discover that the existing video surveillance system is a mess. The original system has been added to and modified over the 20-year life of the property and nothing is labeled or documented. The workmanship of the existing installation is very poor, and the locations where the cables from the existing cameras terminate cannot be easily determined.

1:00 PM: We take a short lunch break and then continue our survey. We have covered only a small portion of the property, and it becomes apparent that several more site visits are likely to be needed. I definitely may have underestimated my fee on this one.

4:00 PM: We finish up for the day, turn in the keys, and begin the commute home. I am leaving feeling a little bit frustrated because even after a full day, I still don't feel that I know what's going on at this property.

6:00 PM: I arrive home and begin to compile my notes from our day's survey work. I also draft a long "to-do" list for our next visit to the site. Because of other commitments, it will be at least another week before we can return to this property again.

Wednesday

7:00 AM: I attend a scheduled webinar put on by a manufacturer of guard force management software. I get dozens of invites to these types of events every month, so I have to be judicious about which ones I accept and which ones I decline. This one is timely because I am considering recommending this type of product for my gated community project.

8:30: I receive a request through the contact form on my website to conduct a security assessment for a distribution center located in Texas. My website is one of my primary sources of business and I receive many inquiries from potential clients each month. I make a note to try to get a proposal off to this person by the end of the day.

9:00 AM: I receive a call from a representative of a condominium that I recently completed a security assessment for. He said that he wants me to delete a few recommendations in my report that he feels won't be well received by homeowners. As a matter of policy, I don't allow clients to dictate what my recommendations should be. I am hired to provide an objective outside opinion and give my best professional advice. I don't delete content just because a particular client representative may not like it. I tell the client I won't delete the recommendations but do agree to rephrase a couple of lines to communicate the same message in a different way.

11:00 AM: I get an email from a risk manager who I have worked with in the past who has recently changed jobs and now works for a large health care services provider. She is now recommending me to do an assessment project for her new company. I have a call with her and her boss to get an understanding of the scope of the project. I tell them that I will review the requirements and then get back to them.

11:30: I prepare a proposal for the distribution center in Texas that I received a website inquiry from earlier. I look at the site using Google maps to get an idea of its size and the type of properties surrounding it. I calculate my total time and travel costs and include them in my fixed-fee proposal. These days, I do all of my projects on a fixed fee basis rather than an hourly plus expenses basis.

12:30 PM: I get back to work on the report for my gated community project. I continue my analysis of incident reports and start to prepare a summary of incidents by type for the previous five years.

6:00 PM: I finally finish my incident report analysis and summary and am now ready to move on to the next phase of the report for my gated community project.

Thursday

7:00 AM: I review the requirements of the health care services provider that I spoke with yesterday. They have about 30 sites spread across five states, none of which are close to me. Because of the number of sites, their location, and my existing backlog of work, I decide that this project is probably not a good fit for me. I send the client an email declining the opportunity and refer them to a larger consulting firm that I know and trust. I hate to turn down work but have learned that it is to everyone's benefit to not stretch yourself too thin.

8:00 AM: I start work on the next phase of the report for my gated community project and discover that there are no good drawings available for this 700-acre site. I begin the process of researching public records and other sources to find usable aerial photographs and survey drawings that I may be able to modify for use in my report. I ponder the fact that due to the proliferation of resources on the internet, this is so much easier now than when I got started as a consultant 35 years ago.

11:00 AM: I know that I will be recommending the use of some type of perimeter protection system for my gated community project, so I contact several manufacturers to get information on their latest products. I attend several trade shows each year to try to stay current with advances in technology, but always do specific research for each project rather than trying to rely on what is in my head.

12:00 PM: I take lunch and check and respond to emails as I eat. I also check a few of my social media accounts and respond to comments on articles I have previously posted.

1:00 PM: I participate in a virtual Executive Committee Meeting for the International Association of Professional Security Consultants (IAPSC). I am currently serving as Immediate Past President of this organization and am asked to sit in on the monthly meetings of the organization's leadership team. I have benefitted greatly from my membership in IAPSC and am happy to give back to the organization however I can.

2:00 PM: I take a break from my project related activities to do a little administrative work. This includes preparing and sending out a few invoices, paying a few bills, and entering transactions in my accounting software. In my early days, I neglected this type of work and was often months behind. As I gained experience, I learned that it was much better to take a little time to stay on top of this work each week, no matter how busy you are with projects.

3:00 PM: I receive a call from another consultant who is wanting to add a technical security consultant to his staff and is looking for recommendations. I tell him that I don't know of anyone presently looking for work and suggest that he try to recruit someone from a systems integrator. It seems that there is always a shortage of good people in this profession.

3:30 PM: I receive a call from a client that I submitted a proposal to several months ago stating that they are ready to move forward with the project. They were not particularly pleased when told that my next available start date was more than 60 days away but were glad to finally get this project underway.

5:00 PM: I get a call from a security equipment manufacturer's representative saying that he will be in town next week and wants to meet me for lunch. I respectfully decline. I deal with several hundred different manufacturers and if I attended every meeting and event I was invited to, I would have time for nothing else.

6:00 PM: I get a call from a woman saying that her privacy was violated when she was using a restroom at a restaurant and was wanting to know if she could sue someone for damages. Apparently, she had read an article on restroom security on my website and thought that I could help. I explained that this was outside of my area of expertise and suggested that she contact a lawyer. The more than 70 articles that I have on my website generate lots of nuisance calls and emails, but also result in many paid consulting assignments.

Friday

7:00 AM: I am notified that my proposal to conduct a security study for a prominent National Football League team has been accepted. I am a football fan and am excited to be associated with this team in even a small way. Most of the work will be conducted remotely so I probably won't get a chance to rub shoulders with the players, but I am thrilled anyway.

8:00 AM: I open my mail and find that I have received yet another thank you letter from a member of a church that I did a pro bono project for a few months earlier. I have received more than a dozen individual letters plus a potted plant expressing thanks for my services. I get great satisfaction from doing pro bono work.

9:00 AM: I get a call from a property manager who manages a retail strip mall that is having security problems. I tell him about my security assessment process and quote him a price. He tells me that he doesn't want an assessment but says "I *want to buy a couple of hours of your time to walk around the property and give me some ideas*". I tell him that I follow a structured security assessment process and that I cannot give advice "off-the-cuff" based on just a quick walk-through. I have found that clients are almost always disappointed with the results of this type of limited engagement. They usually expect the level of detail found in an assessment report, but don't want to go through the assessment process or pay for an assessment.

10:00 AM: I have a Zoom meeting with a client to review a draft of the security system design documents that I prepared for their facility. I was expecting a bit of pushback due to the estimated cost being higher than expected, but to my surprise, they had no objection and even wanted to add additional items to the design.

11:00 AM: I'm back to work on the report for my gated community project. The ability to multitask and flip between projects at a moment's notice is essential once your consulting practice becomes fully established. I sometimes yearn for the very early days in my career when I could concentrate on only one project at a time.

12:00 PM: I reach out to a potential supplier of a key management system for my gated community project. The supplier promptly responds to my request and gives me everything that I need. I am pleasantly surprised as this is definitely the exception rather than the rule when a consultant requests information. Many suppliers only respond after repeated requests and some don't respond at all. I am still baffled as to how disinterested many salespeople seem to be when a consultant is considering recommending their product.

1:00 PM: A person who owns a small apartment building bought my book on multifamily property security and called asking for advice on a specific type of lock hardware. I give him the names of some suppliers who could provide what he needs. I'm happy to provide a limited amount of free advice to people who call or email with just a question or two.

2:00 PM: I review the draft of a security policies and procedures document sent to me by a security manager at one of my clients. The document looks good overall, but I note a few typos and a couple of areas where descriptions could be made clearer. I prepare an email with my comments and send it to the client. Because of the large amount of previous work that this client has given me, I decide not to bill them for the hour that it took me to review this document.

3:00 PM: I order a crime forecast report for my gated community project and spend some time analyzing it. While reports of this type are not infallible, I use them as one part of my overall risk assessment process.

3:30 PM: I create a risk assessment matrix for my gated community project and rank each possible loss event by likelihood and consequences. Over the last 35 years I have developed a number of tools that allow me to do this quickly and consistently. I still feel that many aspects of risk assessment are highly subjective so am always looking for ways to do this better.

5:30 PM: I finish the risk assessment chapter in my report and decide that I have done enough work for the day.

Saturday

7:00 AM: I begin the consultant's findings and recommendations portion of my report for the gated community project. I get some of my best report production work done on Saturdays as there are fewer interruptions, and I can concentrate on my writing.

11:00 AM: I take a break for lunch and read postings on various security forums and groups that I belong to. I don't agree with everything that is being posted, but still find much of the content to be very informative. I particularly enjoy reading about actual experiences that installers and end-users are having with specific security products. Sometimes there is a big difference between manufacturer's claims and reality.

12:00 PM: I continue work on my gated community report and decide that I don't like the order that items are arranged. I reshuffle everything and then continue writing more recommendations. It looks like this report will have more than fifty recommendations in total, a larger number than usual for a project of this type.

3:00 PM: I begin to create the graphics needed to better explain some of the recommendations in my report. These include drawings, photos, and charts. I use at least ten different software tools to create graphics. I don't always remember how to use the features in each program so sometimes need to look things up as I go along. I find graphics to be very helpful in communicating ideas to a client but use them only when needed and not as "filler" to bulk up a report. A pet peeve of mine is a consultant's report that has lots of pictures and charts but conveys very little useful information.

5:00 PM: I stop working on my report for the day. I take a little time to make airline, hotel, and rental car reservations for an assessment project that I have in California later in the month and then decide to take the rest of the weekend off.

Many people considering entering the security consulting field assume that their prior experience in law enforcement, the military, or security management immediately qualifies them to be security consultants. While there are some exceptional individuals who are already fully qualified, the vast majority of people entering the field will need to acquire many new skills in order to succeed as consultants. Failure to recognize this fact is one reason why most new security consultants fail.

Four Areas of Expertise Required

The successful independent security consultant must possess expertise in four separate areas:

Four Areas of Expertise Required

Subject Expertise

Subject expertise is the core expertise possessed by the security consultant in their chosen area of practice. For example, the security management consultant must have expertise in the area of security management, and the technical security consultant must have expertise in physical and electronic security systems. Similarly, forensic security consultants and cybersecurity consultants are each expected to possess expertise in their stated area of practice.

It is assumed that anyone entering the security consulting profession will possess subject expertise in their chosen area of practice.

Consultants whose only previous experience was in the military or law enforcement may find that their skills don't translate well to the private sector and that they will have to adapt them in order to be successful in the business world.

Consulting Expertise

Consulting expertise involves the skills necessary to effectively communicate ideas to a client and to successfully manage a consulting project from start to finish. Consulting expertise includes skills such as interviewing, writing, making presentations, and project management.

A consultant who has subject expertise but lacks consulting skills provides very little value – what good is it to have great command of your subject if you cannot effectively communicate your ideas to your client?

The importance of good writing skills cannot be overstated. Just about every facet of security consulting involves lots of writing, and if you can't write well, or dislike writing, you will face serious challenges as an independent security consultant.

Sales Expertise

Sales expertise involves the skills necessary to consistently generate enough work to support the consulting practice. Sales expertise includes skills such as marketing, business development, making sales calls, writing proposals, and negotiating contracts.

The inability to consistently generate enough work is the leading cause of the failure of new security consulting practices. Consultants who wish to succeed must be able to sell.

Business Expertise

Business expertise involves the skills necessary to profitably run the consulting practice as a business enterprise. Business expertise includes skills such as creating budgets, estimating projects, controlling expenses, bookkeeping and accounting, invoicing, filing tax reports, and other general business management skills.

Consultants that lack business expertise can generate a lot of work and stay very busy, but often get to the end of the year and realize that they are broke, or even worse, deeply in debt.

Evaluating Where You Are At

Each person entering the consulting arena brings along with them a different set of skills. Some new consultants will already have expertise in each of the four areas outlined above and will only have to make a few minor additions to their skill set in order to be successful.

An example would be an experienced security director who previously functioned as an "internal consultant" within their organization, and who also happened to have previous sales experience from a job in college. This person would likely possess all four areas of expertise and would be ideally positioned to quickly succeed as a consultant.

At the other end of the spectrum would be a person who was leaving a job as an engineer at a security systems integration company. While this person would have strong subject skills in the area of technical security, they would probably lack consulting expertise, sales expertise, and business expertise, requiring a much steeper learning curve in order to be successful.

Prospective consultants should make an objective evaluation of their own skill sets to identify areas of weakness. Once identified, a plan should be put into place to correct these weaknesses. Many new consultants shrug off the need to acquire additional skills, thinking that they already have what it takes. They are itching to get started and don't want to stop to take the time to learn anything. These are the consultants that usually fail.

Gaining the Additional Skills That You Need

There are numerous ways in which the prospective consultant can gain the additional skills needed. Here is an example of some resources available to help you to better develop your skills:

- Instructional videos are available on YouTube covering a wide range of topics including sales, marketing presentation techniques, accounting, and many others. The quality of YouTube videos varies, but watching enough different videos on the same topic usually provides excellent results.
- The Small Business Administration (SBA), along with its affiliated organization, SCORE provides numerous free resources including online training videos and local classes. SCORE advisors are also available to provide one-on-one consultation to business owners at no charge.
- Local community colleges often offer classes on topics such as technical writing and presentation skills.
- There are writing coaches and tutors available that can provide individualized instruction to help you further develop your writing skills. Many of these people provide their services at a surprisingly low cost and can often be found on classified advertising websites such as Craigslist.
- Toastmasters International provides an environment to help you to develop your public speaking and presentation skills. There are local Toastmasters Chapters in nearly every major city.
- The International Association of Professional Security Consultants (IAPSC) offers a "Successful Security Consulting" class that provides guidance to the new independent security consultant. These classes are often held in conjunction with major industry trade shows. The IAPSC also holds an annual conference that provides educational sessions on various security consulting topics. You do not need to be an IAPSC member to attend.

- Many experienced independent security consultants are gladly willing to provide mentoring to new security consultants. It is suggested that you identify one or more seasoned consultants that might be willing to serve as your mentor. Membership in the IAPSC is one way to meet other consultants and possibly identify people who would be willing to help.

Some people entering the security consulting profession may think that they can "outsource" activities in the areas where they are weak. For example, a consultant that lacked selling skills might choose to hire someone else to do their selling. Similarly, a consultant who had no business skills might choose to hire someone to manage their business for them

While there is a time and place for the outsourcing of certain functions as your business grows, I feel strongly that the consultant that is dependent on others to provide core business functions operates at a severe disadvantage. I recommend that every consultant take the steps necessary to bolster their skills in the areas where they are weak rather than relying on an outside party.

Formal Education

Conventional wisdom states that having a formal education is a prerequisite to becoming a professional consultant. The expectation is that a beginning consultant possesses at least a bachelor's degree, and that more seasoned consultants possess master's or doctorate degrees.

In the security consulting profession, I have found that the necessity of having a formal education varies greatly depending on the environment in which the consultant operates.

Within traditional Fortune 100 corporations, healthcare establishments, and academic institutions, having a formal education can matter greatly when the client is evaluating security management consultants. Most people on the client's selection committee will probably hold advanced degrees themselves and may look unfavorably upon a candidate that does not have a degree.

On the other hand, the people at most start-up and high-technology companies could care less about degrees – they want someone who can do the job, regardless of the formal education they have received.

Ideally, a person considering a career as an independent security management or forensic consultant would hold a degree in criminal justice or security management, while a person pursuing a career as a cybersecurity consultant would hold a degree in computer science or cybersecurity.

For technical security consultants, I consider having a degree in electrical engineering, computer science, or architecture to be a definite plus, even though only a small percentage of technical security consultants practicing today possess these credentials.

Having an advanced business degree such as a master's in business administration is also advantageous as most security consultants work frequently with the senior management of large companies and must be fluent in the language of business.

With all of the above being said, prospective consultants without degrees should not be discouraged. Many independent security consultants, including myself, hold no degrees, and yet have managed to build very successful security consulting practices.

Past Job Experience

Security consulting is something that is most commonly done at the later stages of one's career after having gained experience in the private security industry, in law enforcement, or in the military.

Most security consultants come from senior leadership roles in their previous organizations. A person rarely comes right out of college and becomes a security consultant, nor establishes a successful practice after having just served a short stint in law enforcement or the military.

The person who is starting an independent security consulting practice typically has at least ten years of previous experience in security or a related field, with twenty years or more of experience being common. That is not to say that a person with less experience couldn't be successful but might face challenges when competing with more seasoned consultants.

The type of experience necessary depends on the practice area in which the prospective consultant intends to operate. People with experience in security management at a private company are usually well-suited to start a security management consulting practice that serves private businesses.

People whose only previous experience was in the military or law enforcement might face greater challenges when starting a practice that served clients in the private sector. On the other hand, a security consultant with a recent military background might definitely have an advantage when starting a practice intended to serve the military or federal government.

Consultants who intend to operate as specialists within a certain segment of the industry are best served when their past experience is in the area of their specialty. For example, a consultant who wanted to specialize in hospital security would most certainly benefit from having previously worked as a security director at one or more well-known hospitals.

Forensic security consultants should have some practical experience in the areas in which they profess to be experts – it's difficult to claim to be an expert at something you haven't done yourself. For example, a consultant with a background only in retail security might face tough questions from the opposing attorney when testifying as an expert on a multifamily apartment building case (*so, Mr. Expert, how many security assessments for apartment buildings have you personally conducted in the past?)*

When just starting out, your past job experience is very important, as you have few, if any, past consulting projects that can be used as references. As you get more and more projects under your belt, your employment history becomes less and less important, as clients tend to give more weight to recent consulting project experience than they do to past employment history.

Industry Certifications

There are numerous certification programs available within the security profession. These include the Certified Protection Professional (CPP), Physical Security Professional (PSP), and Professional Certified Investigator (PCI) credentials offered by ASIS International; the Certified Information Systems Security Professional (CISSP) issued by $(ISC)^2$; the Certified Healthcare Protection Administrator (CHPA) offered by the International Association for Healthcare Security and Safety; the Certified Security Consultant (CSC) certification offered by the IAPSC, and a multitude of others.

While many of these certifications are well-thought of within the industry itself, they can be meaningless to the average person. Most clients seeking security consulting services have no idea what these certifications are and probably don't care one way or the other if a consultant has a specific certification or not.

One exception is when a client's purchasing department is drafting a formal request-for-proposal (RFP) for security consulting services and does some prior research to determine what credentials are available in the industry. In these cases, you will often see the purchasing department include a requirement for the lead consultant on the project to possess either a CPP, PSP, or CISSP certification depending on the project's scope of work.

The bottom line: having at least one of the primary certifications related to your area of practice such as the CPP, CISSP, CSC, or PSP can be beneficial. When pursuing certain projects, certain certifications may be mandatory. Having additional certifications can't hurt, but probably isn't necessary.

However, if you do obtain many certifications, I suggest that you limit the number of them used on your signature line to three or less. I have found that having a large number of letters behind your name makes you look pompous and can actually be a turn-off to some people.

Personal Qualities

Last, but certainly not least, are the personal qualities required to succeed as an independent security consultant. These are as listed below and presented in no particular order:

- Self-confidence.
- Honesty and integrity.
- Strong work ethic.
- Highly motivated and a self-starter.
- Positive, optimistic attitude.
- Conscious of appearance and possess good grooming habits.
- Good listener.
- Respectful of all people regardless of class.
- Problem-solver not problem-creator.
- Persistent and unwilling to quit until they succeed.

Chapter 4 - Planning Your Consulting Practice

Starting an independent security consulting practice requires lots of careful planning. This chapter provides guidelines on some of the many things that need to be considered prior to the opening of your new business.

Determine Your Specific Area of Practice

One of the first and most important things that you can do is to determine the specific areas in which you intend to practice as a security consultant. This involves deciding exactly what types of services you will provide, and who you will provide them to. To help you reach this determination, you should answer the following questions:

1 - What Type of Consultant Do I Want to Be?

Security Management Consultant

Technical Security Consultant

Forensic Security Consultant

Cybersecurity Consultant

Other Type of Security Consultant

2 - What Types of Clients Do I Want to Serve?

Apartments and Condominiums

Architects

Attorneys

Cannabis Facilities

Casinos

Colleges and Universities

Corporate Headquarters Facilities

Courthouses

Engineers

Federal Government

Hospitals and Healthcare Institutions

Hotels and Hospitality Venues

Law Enforcement Agencies

Libraries

Military

Museums and Cultural Institutions

Non-Profits and Charitable Organizations

Parking Facilities

Private Residences

Public Schools

Retail Stores

Shopping Centers

Shopping Malls

Stadiums and Sporting Venues

State and Local Government

Warehouse and Distribution Centers

Other Clients

3 - What Types of Services Will I Offer?

Contract Negotiation

CPTED Planning

Crime Analysis

Design Review

Design Standard Development

Expert Witness Testimony

Guard Force Training

Penetration Testing

Policies and Procedures Development

Project Management

Proposal Review

Recruitment Services

Security Assessments

Security Awareness Training

Security Director as a Service (SDaaS)

Security Plan Development

Security System Design

Security System Testing

Specification Writing

Technical Surveillance Countermeasures (TSCM).

Travel Security

Workplace Violence Training

Other Services

Once you have answered these questions, draft a statement that summarizes your area of practice and the services that you will provide. Here are some examples:

> *I am a security management consultant that serves hospitals and healthcare institutions. I provide security assessments, policies and procedures development, and security awareness training.*
>
> *I am a technical security consultant that works for architects and engineers to design security systems for courthouses, law enforcement agencies, and state and local government agencies.*
>
> *I am a forensic security consultant that serves attorneys. I provide expert witness services in cases involving retail stores and shopping malls.*

I am a cybersecurity consultant that serves colleges and universities. I perform IT security assessments, conduct penetration tests, and develop IT security policies and procedures.

Many prospective security consultants may find statements like the ones above to be far too restrictive. They have a wide range of skills and want to offer them to as many clients as possible.

While there is certainly nothing to prevent you from offering an expansive range of services to many different types of clients, I urge you, particularly at the start of your practice, to have a fairly narrow practice area. This allows you to concentrate your marketing efforts on a specific type of prospective client and prevents you from losing your focus on who you should be selling to and why. As an old saying goes: *"if you try to be everything to everybody, you will end up being nothing to no one"*.

Keep in mind that your area of practice will likely evolve and change over time. As you get more experience, you may see areas where clients need services that you are not currently offering and may choose to expand your service offerings to meet this need.

For example, after you complete a security assessment for a company, you may see the need for this client to retain the services of an "on-call security director", sometimes called Security Director as a Service (SDaaS). This is a service that you had not originally thought to provide but are certainly qualified to deliver. You may choose to add this service to your list of service offerings.

On the other hand, you may find that one or more of the services that you originally intended to offer are simply not selling. For example, one of the services that you intended to offer may have been CPTED planning for schools, but when selling these services, you discover that essentially the same services are being provided by local law enforcement agencies for free. Since you stand little or no chance of selling these services, you may wish to drop them from your service offerings and add a new service instead.

So, while you will always have the opportunity to expand or change your areas of practice and service offerings later, you should decide what you initially want to offer on the day you start your practice. This will allow you to focus your marketing efforts and keep you on track.

Naming Your Consulting Practice

What to name your business is an important decision and one that should not be taken lightly. Your business name can define who you are and what services that you provide and is the first step in establishing a brand for your company.

The simplest and easiest thing to do is to simply name the business using your entire personal name. Examples would be "John Doe Consultants" or "Sally Doe Consultants". Some consultants, anticipating the use of employees or subcontractors, add the words "and Associates" to the end of their name, creating a name like "John Doe & Associates".

The second choice is to use only a portion of your name, usually your last name, in your business name. Examples would be "Doe Services" or "Doe Forensic Consultants". In my case, I started out using my full name, "Michael Silva Consultants", but shortened the name to just "Silva Consultants" a few years later.

The third choice is to use a trade name as your business name. These are also sometimes called "assumed names" or "fictitious names". Examples would be "Acme Security Consultants", "Total Security Advisors", or "Ace Computer Forensics".

Here are some things to think about when choosing a name for your consulting practice:

- If you are already well-known and respected within the security community, you may want to capitalize on your personal name. People who were previously a security director at a large corporation or who held high-ranking positions in law enforcement or the military can often benefit from the "brand-equity" that already exists around their name.

- People who have names that are long or difficult to spell or pronounce may wish to think twice before using their personal name as their business name.
- Check to see if the business name you are considering is already in use, both in your market area, and elsewhere in the world. This seems pretty obvious, but it is surprising how many times someone names a business and then finds a short time later that there are already several other businesses using the same name.
- Picking a name that specifically defines your practice area is a two-edged sword: it can offer a powerful advantage when selling to your chosen market but can be a severe disadvantage should you choose to sell into other markets. For example, the name "Hospital Security Consultants" would be great for selling to hospitals but would probably be a handicap if you later chose to sell your services to public schools.
- Check the availability of internet domain names available to match the business name that you are considering. (See Establishing an Internet Domain below.)
- People often abbreviate their company name using a combination of letters. For example, the company name "Total Security Advisors" might be abbreviated as "TSA". Consider this when choosing your name so that any abbreviation used works for you and not against you.
- Try to avoid using names that suggest that you are anything other than a consultant. For example, the name "Acme Security Services" could be the name of a security consulting firm but could also be the name of an alarm company or guard service.
- If you are not a licensed professional engineer, don't use the words "engineer" or "engineering" in your company name.

- Should you ever wish to sell your consulting practice in the future, having a name like "John Doe Consultants" might be a disadvantage, as it is unlikely that the buyer would want to continue to use your name once you are gone.

The laws in most states require that you register your business name unless you are using your full personal name as the business name. This process is known as filing to use a fictitious name, assumed name, trade name or doing business as (DBA) name. Check with your state and local government agencies to see what is required to register your business name.

Registering a business name is usually done on a state-by-state basis and registering your name in one state does not necessarily prevent someone else from using it in another state. If you wish to protect your name on a national basis, it may be possible to trademark it. If this is something that you wish to consider, it is suggested that you consult with your legal advisor.

Establishing an Internet Domain

The internet has become a vital part of our personal and professional life and is used by most people continuously throughout the day. Any independent security consultant who wishes to be successful needs to have an effective presence on the internet and be uniquely identifiable as an expert in their chosen field of practice.

The first step in creating an internet identity is to obtain a unique domain name for your consulting practice. This domain should be used in the URL for your website, as well as in your personal email address. For example, my domain name is "silvaconsultants.com", my website URL is "www.silvaconsultants.com", and my email address is "mikes@silvaconsultants.com".

Ideally, your internet domain name should match or closely resemble your company name. In my case, my company name is "Silva Consultants", so the match is perfect. Consulting firms who have a long or difficult to spell name may choose to use a combination of letters as their domain name instead of the full business name. For example, "Schwartzenbaum Technical Security Consultants" might consider using "stsc.com" as their domain name.

Another strategy is to use a phrase that describes one of your services as your domain name. For example, a forensic security consultant might choose to use the domain name of "securityexpertwitness.com", when their actual company name is something else.

The system used to establish domain names is actually quite technical, but in simplified terms, domain names consist of two parts: a name, and an extension. In the case of my domain name, "silvaconsultants" is the name, and ".com" is the extension.

For many years, only seven extensions were available, and most business users were assigned the ".com" extension. Today, there are over 300 custom extensions available, giving you countless options for creating a domain name. However, most mainstream businesses still continue to prefer the ".com" extension, and if your name is available with this extension, it is probably the best one to use.

Domain names are available from companies that provide web hosting and email services. Most companies offer a look-up tool on their website that allows you to check various combinations of names and extensions to see if the name that you want to use is already taken. If it is, the tool will suggest other names and extensions that are close to the one that you want.

Most domain names are available for only a small annual registration fee, usually $20 or less per year. In some cases, the annual fee for the domain name is free if you use the company to provide your web hosting services.

Some very popular or catchy domain names have been acquired by resellers and are sold for unbelievably high prices, often costing tens of thousands or even millions of dollars. It should go without saying that acquiring a domain name of this type would not make sense for even the most successful of security consultants.

It is my opinion that having the correct domain name is so important that beginning consultants might want to consider choosing a name for their business based on the availability of a suitable domain name rather than the other way around.

Establishing Your Visual Image

A consulting firm's visual image is conveyed to the world by various means, including brochures, stationery, business cards, report covers, and websites. A visual image is created by the various graphical elements that you use, including text fonts, colors, textures, logos, and other elements.

It is recommended that a consistent visual image be used throughout all of your marketing materials and on all of the work products that you produce. The same visual image should also be used on your website. The following is suggested:

- The overall appearance of your materials should reflect a professional image and not be gaudy or overstated. When in doubt, take the conservative approach.
- A limited number of different fonts and color combinations should be used. A maximum of two to three different fonts, three to four different font sizes, and three to five different colors is suggested. Having eight different fonts and ten different colors on the same page looks amateurish.
- A logo, if used, should be simple and elegant. The logo should be scalable to permit its use on materials both very large and very small.
- All graphical elements should be capable of being used on websites, blogs, and social media sites. Using fonts that are not widely available can create problems.

The proliferation of graphics and desktop publishing programs has made everyone think that they are a graphics designer. Unless you have proven skills in this area, it is recommended that you hire a professional designer to assist you in establishing your visual image.

Retain Qualified Professional Advisors

It is strongly recommended that you identify and retain qualified professional advisors prior to the start of your consulting practice. This would include an attorney and a Certified Public Accountant (CPA).

You should explain to your professional advisors that you are starting your practice and want to establish a long-term ongoing relationship with them. These advisors should be used to help answer questions when you are starting your practice (should I incorporate my business, what type of contract should I use, should I do my accounting using the cash or accrual method, etc.), plus be available to answer questions on an on-call basis as you go along.

For example, as you go about your consulting activities, you will be presented with contracts and other legal documents that your client wishes you to sign. It's nice to have the ability to have these documents reviewed by an attorney who is already familiar with you and your practice.

There is a tendency for beginning consultants to try to be their own accountant or lawyer, and to use the internet as their sole source of legal and accounting advice. In my opinion, this is foolish. Spending a little money on professional advisors up front can actually be cheaper in the long run and help you to avoid serious trouble.

Choose Your Business Structure

There are four types of business structures that are commonly used to establish a consulting practice. These are the Sole Proprietorship, Partnership, Limited Liability Company (LLC), and S Corporation. Each business structure has different legal and tax implications.

If you intend to operate outside of the state in which you are located, certain types of business structures (such as S Corporations and LLCs) may require that you register as a foreign corporation in the other states in which you do business. If you do business in many states, this can involve a significant amount of time and expense.

Most independent security consultants that I know operate either as a Sole Proprietorship or as an LLC. It is recommended that you consult with both your legal advisor and accounting advisor before choosing the business structure that you will use.

Business Licenses

Independent security consultants are required to have business licenses. These would be the same type of license that would be required for a bakery, florist or any other type of business.

The specific requirements for licensing vary from state to state and city to city. In some states, all licensing is done at the state level, while in other states, licensing may also be required at the county, parish, or city level.

Business licenses can usually be obtained easily by simply filling out a few forms and paying a fee. This can often be done completely online.

Professional Licenses

In the majority of states, the security consulting firm is only required to get a general business license as described above. However, in some states, security consulting is considered to be a regulated profession and requires professional licensing in addition to a general business license.

This type of licensing is much harder to obtain, and often requires that both the consulting firm and the people doing the consulting work have special licenses. A sole practitioner would usually be required to obtain two licenses: one as a company owner, and one as the consultant who is doing the work. Obtaining either type of license can require a background check, proof of experience, and the taking of a test. A specific amount of insurance coverage and a surety bond may also be required.

As of the date of this writing, the states that require professional include:

Nevada

The State of Nevada requires a professional license to "engage in the business or advertise his or her business" as a security consultant. Interestingly, there is no specific licensing category for security consultants; in order to perform consulting, you must obtain a license as a private investigator or private patrol company.

Virginia

The State of Virginia requires a professional license to "design or consult in the design of any electronic security equipment to an end user".

This requirement would definitely apply to technical security consultants and could be broadly interpreted to also apply to security management consultants who provide any type of advice concerning electronic security systems.

Professional licensing laws are constantly changing, so you should always check the laws in the states in which you intend to operate.

Technical security consultants who design and specify security systems sometimes operate in a grey area when it comes to professional licensing laws. In some places, this type of work may be considered "engineering", and as such, must be performed by or under the direct supervision of a licensed professional engineer.

Becoming a professional engineer usually requires that the applicant have an engineering degree from an accredited college or university, work under the direction of an already licensed engineer for a four-year period, and to take a rigorous licensing test.

Some states allow technical security consultants to operate without becoming licensed as a professional engineer provided that they do not call themselves "engineers" or say that they are providing "engineering services". Other states are stricter, and technically require that anyone doing design work be registered as a professional engineer. Technical security consultants should determine the specific licensing laws in the states that they intend to operate.

Regardless of state licensing laws, certain clients (such as government agencies) may require that all drawings and specifications, including those for security system designs, be prepared under the supervision of a licensed professional engineer and be appropriately stamped.

Even if not always required, having a professional engineer license provides additional credibility that may be valued by some clients and can offer a marketing advantage in some situations. Having an engineering license can also make additional avenues of liability insurance available to the consultant. For these reasons, I would strongly encourage technical consultants who have the education and experience necessary to become licensed as engineers take the steps to become licensed.

State and Local Taxes

Nearly every state, city, or county imposes some type of tax on the business activities that occur within their jurisdiction. This tax is usually based on revenue, but can also be based on number of employees, square footage of business space being rented, or other factors.

In many cases, obtaining a license in a jurisdiction automatically registers you to pay taxes, and tax forms will be sent to you without requiring any action on your part. In other cases, you must separately register with a tax agency in order to pay taxes. Taxes can be due on a monthly, quarterly or annual basis depending on the agency

Some jurisdictions may require the independent security consultant to collect sales tax on any sales made, while in other jurisdictions, professional services such as consulting are tax exempt.

As with licensing laws, the only way to be certain about what is required is to check with the appropriate agencies in the jurisdictions in which you intend to operate. Consultants who operate over a large geographical area and who do work in many cities can end up with large numbers of different tax forms that they must submit each reporting period. Here is when it is beneficial to have a qualified accounting advisor at your disposal to help guide you through the reporting process.

Some consultants choose to get licensed and pay taxes only in their home state and ignore the licensing and tax laws in other states in which they work. While you could probably get away with this for a while, it will eventually catch up with you and is definitely not recommended.

Income Taxes

When you work as an employee, taxes are usually deducted from your paycheck by your employer. These taxes may include Federal Income Tax, Social Security, Medicare, and other state and local taxes on income.

When you are an independent security consultant, you are your own employer. Except under special circumstances, taxes are not withheld from the income that you receive from clients, and you are responsible for reporting and paying your own taxes.

Many new business owners make the mistake of thinking that all the money that they receive from clients is theirs to keep and spend, when in fact, up to 35% or more of this money is actually tax money. They get to the end of the year and find that they may owe thousands of dollars in taxes and have no means to pay them.

To avoid this trap, the law requires that self-employed people make quarterly tax payments based on their estimated income. Simply stated, this involves estimating what your total annual income will be, and figuring out how much tax will be due. This amount is then divided by four to arrive at the amount of tax that must be paid each quarter. When it comes time to file your taxes at the end of the year, the total amount of estimated tax paid should be close to the total taxes due, usually resulting in a refund or the payment of only a small amount of additional tax.

The form used to calculate, and file estimated tax payments with the Internal Revenue Service is Form 1040-ES. This covers Federal taxes. Most states and other jurisdictions that collect income tax have similar forms available that allow estimated tax payments for state and local taxes to be paid. Your accounting advisor should be consulted if you have any questions regarding the filing of estimated tax payments.

It is suggested that you compare the amount that you figured as your estimated annual income with your actual income at least on a quarterly basis. This can give you an early warning that your estimate was inaccurate and help you to avoid surprises at the end of the year. For example, if you estimated $150,000 in annual income, and on

April 1st you have already earned $70,000, you may wish to increase the amount of your estimated tax payments.

Employer Identification Number

All independent security consultants should obtain an employer identification number (EIN) from the Internal Revenue Service, even if they do not plan on hiring any employees at this time. While sole proprietors can use their personal Social Security Number (SSN) instead of an EIN on many tax forms, it conveys a more professional appearance if you use an EIN. Many consultants would also prefer not to have their personal SSN on business-related documents. An EIN is available at no charge.

Almost every client will request a Form W-9 before making any type of payment to you. Form W-9 gives your client your taxpayer identification number (either EIN or SSN), indicates your business structure, and confirms that your payments are not subject to tax withholdings.

Consultants should be familiar with Form W-9 and be prepared to submit this form any time that they take on a new client. Form W-9 can be downloaded as an editable PDF file from the IRS at no charge.

Business Insurance

All independent security consultants need to have business insurance. The purpose of having this insurance is to provide protection for the business and the personal assets of the owner. In addition, a majority of clients will require that any consultant that they are considering have specific types and amounts of insurance coverage before they can be hired.

The types of business insurance needed by the consultant can include:

General Liability Insurance

General Liability (GL) insurance provides coverage against claims such as property damage, bodily injury, personal injury and other types of claims that occur as a result of the operation of your business. GL insurance can also cover the cost of defending you against lawsuits related to the claims outlined above.

GL insurance does not provide any coverage related to automobiles or other vehicles that you use in your business. GL insurance also does not provide coverage against any professional mistakes that you make or liability that occurs as a result of your errors or omissions.

Commercial Auto Insurance

Commercial auto insurance is similar to personal auto insurance but offers increased limits of coverage and greater flexibility. Commercial auto insurance can be required when vehicles are owned by a company or operated by one of its employees.

Independent security consultants who use their personal vehicle in conjunction with their consulting practice may or may not need commercial auto insurance depending on their circumstances. In some cases, a personal auto policy may specifically prohibit the use of a vehicle for business purposes. In other cases, a personal auto policy may not provide the coverage limits requested by clients, making it necessary to purchase a commercial policy.

Professional Liability (Errors & Omission) Insurance

Professional Liability (PL) insurance, also known as Errors and Omissions insurance, provides protection against claims concerning alleged mistakes made by the consultant, bad advice that the consultant gives, and oversights or omissions on the part of the consultant. PL also covers the cost of defending you against lawsuits related to the claims outlined above.

Most independent security consultants have no difficulty in obtaining general liability insurance and commercial auto insurance. These policies are available from a large number of different underwriters, usually at a reasonable cost.

Professional liability insurance is a different matter. As of the date of this writing, there were relatively few avenues of professional liability insurance available to the independent security consultant, and as a result, it can be hard to obtain and is somewhat expensive.

It is recommended that a qualified insurance broker be consulted prior to the start of your security consulting practice to review the types of insurance that you may require and your options for purchasing the necessary coverage.

The cost of insurance is directly linked to the coverage limits requested. More often than not, the independent security consultant will find it necessary to purchase higher coverage limits in order to meet the needs of clients. For example, a consultant may choose to have $1,000,000 limits on their general liability, professional liability, and commercial auto policies, but learn that clients in their chosen area of practice require a minimum of $3,000,000 of coverage. This consultant may find it difficult or impossible to do business unless a policy with higher limits is obtained.

You may encounter situations where a majority of your clients find the limits of your policies acceptable, but you have one specific client who requests higher limits. For example, you may have $1,000,000 in coverage but find that a specific client is asking for $3,000,000.

In some cases, you can convince the client to accept the coverage that you have, but if this doesn't work, you may need to increase the limits of your policies or purchase an "umbrella" policy just for this specific client. Umbrella policies can provide coverage of the amount between the limits of your underlying policy and the limits that your client is requesting.

Sometimes, the client will require that you maintain insurance not only while the work is being performed, but also for several years afterwards. You need to factor these costs into your proposal if you are purchasing an umbrella policy just to meet the requirements of a specific project.

Unfortunately, you may come across cases where the insurance coverage requested by a potential client is unobtainable or prohibitively expensive. I have had to walk away from projects in the past where it just didn't make good business sense to buy the insurance needed to comply with the client's requirements.

As proof that you have insurance coverage, most clients will request that you submit a "Certificate of Insurance" (COI) along with your proposal or prior to the issuance of a contract. The COI specifies the types of insurance policies that you have and your coverage limits. The COI may also specify that the client is an "additional insured", meaning that the client is covered by the insurance policies in addition to yourself.

The COI is typically requested from the insurance broker that sold you your policies. COIs are often needed on short notice, so having a broker that can respond quickly to your requests is important. The process for obtaining a COI and the expected turnaround time should be discussed when selecting an insurance broker.

When responding to a request-for-proposal or negotiating a contract with a client, it is strongly recommended that your insurance broker review any contract language concerning insurance and indemnification. This can prevent you from unintentionally agreeing to provide insurance coverage that is outside of the scope of your present policies.

Vendor Compliance Management Services

Some clients use what are known as "vendor compliance management" services to help ensure that all vendors meet all necessary compliance requirements, such as insurance coverage, licenses, and certifications. These services are commonly used by clients that manage commercial and multifamily residential properties.

To work for a client that uses these services, you must first register with the vendor compliance company and pay an annual subscription fee. You then submit documents such as certificates of insurance, copies of licenses, and other information to the compliance company. Once you have complied with all requirements, the compliance company notifies both you and the client that you are "approved" to work at the property.

The compliance company keeps close watch on the expiration dates of your licenses and insurance and will notify you when they are about to expire. If you fail to submit updated documents, they will notify you and your client that you are "out of compliance" and can do no further work at the property until the matter is resolved.

There are a number of different vendor compliance companies, and different clients may use different ones. This may require you to pay several annual subscription fees. I do a lot of work in the multifamily housing industry and am required to maintain subscriptions to at least three separate vendor compliance companies at the present time.

Sometimes, you will get a single project that requires you to subscribe to a vendor management company. When that project is completed, there is always a question as to whether or not you should continue your subscription in case that client gives you future work – or to drop your subscription and reapply when it is needed again.

Accounting

Having an accurate accounting system is vital to enable you to track sales and expenses and quickly determine the financial condition of your business at any time. Operating a consulting business without a reliable accounting system in place is like driving a car blindfolded.

It is possible to do your accounting manually using a paper journal and ledger, or by using a computer spreadsheet. These methods can work when your consulting practice is small but become cumbersome to use as your business grows.

I recommend that consultants use professional accounting software, such as QuickBooks, starting at the very beginning of their consulting practice. This allows you to use the same system throughout the life of your business and avoids having to transition between systems as you grow.

Professional accounting software allows you to create budgets and forecasts, track time and expenses, create invoices and statements, and run financial reports of all types. This software allows the consultant to track financial activities on a daily basis and to determine quickly how the business is doing financially.

While the average person can probably install and use accounting software on their own, it is suggested that an accounting advisor be hired to assist with the initial setup of the accounting system. The accounting advisor should be asked to provide guidance on what accounting methods should be used, what types of accounts should be created, and how tax rates and other variables within the system should be entered.

Once the system is set up, you should be able to perform most daily accounting activities without requiring further assistance. However, if an issue arises, the accounting advisor will already be familiar with your business and accounting system and should be able to answer any questions quickly.

Your accounting advisor should also be consulted to help with filling out various types of tax forms and in helping you to prepare your annual tax returns.

Bank Account

Your consulting practice should have its own commercial bank account in the name of your business. Using a personal bank account for your business is not recommended.

Once established, the business bank account should be used exclusively for business purposes. All revenue received by the business should be deposited into this account, and all expenses paid by the business should come out of this account.

Personal expenses should never be paid directly out of your business bank account. When necessary to draw funds for personal use, a business check made payable to you personally should be written. This type of transaction is normally called an "Owners Draw" and is posted in the accounting system as such. This check can then be cashed or deposited into your personal bank account to enable you to pay personal expenses. This type of transaction is the way that most self-employed people receive their "paycheck".

The most basic type of business account is the business checking account. Business savings accounts, as well as combined checking/savings accounts are also available. Savings accounts, as well as some checking accounts, pay interest on funds held within the account.

Many clients now pay their invoices using the direct deposit method. Most direct deposits are made through an Automated Clearing House so are often called "ACH deposits". To receive these deposits, you will need to provide the bank routing number and account number for your account, so it is useful to have these numbers at your fingertips. Some clients may also pay by electronic wire transfer and having these numbers is also necessary to complete this type of transaction.

Accepting Credit Cards

Increasingly, both small and large businesses, as well as some government agencies, are using business credit cards to pay their bills. In some cases, payment can be received on the spot for consulting services rendered, eliminating the need to send an invoice and wait to receive a check. I am finding that more and more of my clients use business credit cards as their preferred method of payment.

To accept credit card payments, you need to establish a merchant account at your bank or use a credit card processing service. Some providers of accounting software also provide the ability to accept credit card payments through their platform. There are also popular digital payment platforms that allow users to send and receive money electronically. These were intended primarily for personal use but can also be used for business purposes.

There is normally a fee associated with each credit card transaction. These fees typically range between 2% and 4% of the transaction and can quickly add up over the course of a year. To minimize these fees, try to encourage your clients to pay by check or direct deposit rather than with a credit card.

Payment Processing Services

Some clients use third-party payment processing services to streamline their payments to vendors and suppliers. These processing services most commonly make payments to vendors using the direct deposit (ACH) method but can also send checks.

The payment processing service charges a processing fee to make the payment. This fee is typically about 2% and is paid by the vendor receiving the payment. You usually don't have a choice about paying this fee when working with clients that use this type of service, but you should be aware of it in advance so that it doesn't come as a surprise.

Using Credit Cards

A credit card is needed to make travel reservations, rent a car, and to pay for miscellaneous expenses. If at all possible, you should use a separate credit card to make purchases related to your consulting practice. This credit card should be used exclusively for business and not used to make personal purchases. The statement for the credit card should be paid in full each month with a check drawn on your business checking account

When starting your practice, it may not be possible to obtain a credit card in your business name. If this is the case, you may wish to obtain an additional card in your personal name but use it only for business purposes.

Office Space

When I started my consulting practice in 1985, it was considered almost mandatory for a consultant to rent commercial office space. I operated out of my tiny apartment for the first several months, then rented my first office. As my practice grew and I began to hire employees, I continued to rent larger offices, moving several times until I eventually joined an international consulting firm which had plush offices in a downtown high-rise office building. When I left this firm to resume my independent practice, I decided that I would go back to working from home, coming full circle from where I had started.

Due to advances in technology, changes in work culture, and the lingering impact of the pandemic of 2020, work from home is now the rule rather than the exception in many organizations. This is particularly true in the consulting profession, where much of the work is done at the client's location or can be accomplished easily from almost anywhere using just a cell phone and a laptop computer.

Today, many of even the very largest security consulting firms operate using employees working from home. These employees are typically placed at strategic locations throughout the country, giving the company a large geographical footprint at minimal expense. These firms may still have a physical office located somewhere that serves as their headquarters, but the vast majority of their employees work from home.

When starting your consulting practice, you will likely find it to be most practical and cost effective to work from home. The important thing is to establish a comfortable environment in which you can work productively.

Having a separate room in your home that can be used as an office is ideal. This allows you to arrange furniture and equipment in a manner that allows you to operate efficiently. Distractions can also be avoided by closing the door and you have the ability to create a clear distinction between your personal living space and your workspace.

If a separate room for an office is not available, you can still work from home, but it may be more challenging.

There may be circumstances when working from home is not an option, requiring that commercial office space be rented. Examples of these types of circumstances can include:

- You don't have adequate space in your home to create a home office. For example, technical security consultants may require additional space due to their need to work with architectural and engineering drawings. This can require equipment such as drafting tables, drawing storage racks or cabinets, plotters, and scanning equipment – all of which take up space.
- Operating a business in your home is prohibited by zoning laws, lease agreements, or homeowner's association bylaws.
- The conditions in your home create too many distractions making it difficult or impossible for you to work effectively.

- You have difficulty in deciding when you are at work and when you are not at work. Some people need physical separation between their personal space and their workspace in order to be productive and happy.
- You have a frequent need to meet with clients or business associates and you lack adequate meeting space in your home or feel uncomfortable having business guests in your private home.
- There is a marketing advantage in being located close to your client base. For example, a technical security consultant who serves architects may find it advantageous to have an office in the heart of the city close to where most major architectural firms are located.
- You are working on consulting assignments involving classified information that requires that all work be performed in government-approved secure facilities,

Renting commercial office space on an ongoing basis can greatly increase your operating expenses. Rent must be paid month after month, year after year, even when business is slow or when clients fail to pay you on time.

There are services that exist that offer an alternative to renting commercial office space. These services provide what are known as "coworking spaces" that are made available to members for a monthly fee.

Members typically have access to a number of amenities including working spaces, conference rooms, teleconferencing equipment, internet service, copy machines, and a break room. Some facilities also provide a receptionist who can answer your telephone, receive your packages, and greet your guests. Some coworking spaces also provide networking opportunities and offer wellness facilities such as gyms.

Coworking spaces typically require a monthly membership fee, plus a fee to rent a desk on either a daily or monthly basis. There are usually additional fees required to rent conference rooms or utilize other facilities. Some coworking spaces offer a membership package that is all inclusive and gives members access to everything for a single monthly fee. Coworking spaces can be ideal for the independent security consultant who chooses to have an office outside of the home on either a part-time or full-time basis.

When considering what type of office arrangement to have, be sure that you are making your decision based on business needs rather than your ego. While it may be nice to have first-class office space in a downtown high-rise building, 99% of your clients will never know or even care about what type of office space that you occupy. Putting yourself in financial jeopardy just to impress your colleagues or a few salespeople doesn't make sense.

Office Equipment

It will be necessary to provide equipment for your home office. Many consultants who are starting an office at home may already have some or all of the equipment necessary. Consultants who choose to rent an office may find that their office suite already comes furnished with at least part of the equipment that they will need.

Each person will have their own personal preferences when it comes to equipment. The important thing is to have all the items necessary to allow you to work comfortably and productively. Here are the minimum items that are typically needed in the office of a security management consultant or forensic security consultant:

- Desk.
- Executive office chair.
- Worktable.
- File cabinet.
- Bookshelf.
- Personal computer with keyboard, mouse, speakers, and a video monitor.
- Second video monitor (optional, but highly recommended.)
- Webcam for teleconferencing.
- External microphone for computer (if not included in webcam)

- Uninterruptible power supply (UPS) for computers and monitors.
- External disk drive for back-ups.
- All-in-one printer, scanner, and copy machine. (Or separate devices that provide the equivalent functions.)
- Label printer.
- Document shredder.

Technical security consultants who work with full-sized drawings may also have a need for items such as a plotter, drafting table, and drawing storage racks. Cybersecurity consultants may also have the need for specialized test equipment related to their work.

Because of the sensitive client information that security consultants work with, they should equip their home office with the same type of security measures that they would recommend for their clients that face a similar level of security risk.

Ironically, many security consultants don't take their own security seriously and often have conditions at their home office that they would severely criticize if they were conducting a security assessment for a client.

Business Software

Most of the work created by the independent security consultant will be done on a computer using software of various types. When starting your consulting business, it will be necessary to make sure that you have all the software that is needed. Here are the common types of software typically used by the consultant:

- Word processing program, such as Microsoft Word.
- Spreadsheet program, such as Microsoft Excel.
- Email/calendar/contact program, such as Microsoft Outlook.
- Presentation software, such as Microsoft PowerPoint.
- Drawing/diagramming software, such as Microsoft Visio.
- PDF file creator/editor, such as Adobe Acrobat.

- Photo editing program, such as Adobe Photoshop.
- Accounting software, such as Intuit QuickBooks.
- Video conferencing software, such as Microsoft Teams or Zoom.

Most technical security consultants will also need computer-aided-drafting (CAD) and/or building information management (BIM) software to create security system design drawings. Some security management consultants may also choose to use CAD software to create drawings and illustrations for their reports.

In each category of software, there is usually one brand-name product that is considered to be the industry standard. For instance, in the word processing category, Microsoft Word is considered to be the standard. There are then usually one or more alternative products that are available for free or at a much lower cost. For example, Google Docs is a cloud-based program that provides most of the functionality of Word and is available for free. Similarly, paint.net provides most of the basic functions that Photoshop does but can be downloaded at no charge.

The decision to use brand-name software or a less expensive alternative depends on your circumstances. If you have already gained proficiency in using a particular brand of software at your previous job, it may be easier to continue to use that same software in your consulting practice. Also, if there is a need for you to work collaboratively on documents with other consultants or your clients, it can be advantageous to use the same brand of software that they are using.

Over the years, I have tried many various types of alternative software that claimed to be fully compatible with brand-name products. In nearly every case, I found that when transferring documents between programs, the translation was OK, but not completely perfect, often requiring some minor reformatting.

In my personal consulting practice, I have chosen to stick with brand-name products and spend a significant amount of money per year on software. You may find that for your needs, less expensive alternative products will work just fine.

Mailing Address

Your consulting practice will need a mailing address. If you are renting a commercial office space, your mailing address would typically be the physical address of your office.

Consultants who operate out of their home are sometimes reluctant to use their home address as their mailing address for privacy reasons. In these cases, they often choose to get a post office box at either their local United States Postal Service (USPS) post office or at a private mailbox service.

When using a USPS box, your mailing address is a PO Box number. An example would be as follows:

XYZ Consultants
PO Box 1234
Seattle, WA 98101

Some consultants feel that using a PO Box number as their mailing address is unprofessional and sends the wrong message to their clients and choose to use a private mailbox service instead.

Using a private mailbox number allows you to use a street address and box number rather than just a PO Box address. The way that the box number is formatted can give the illusion that it is a suite number rather than box number. An example would be as follows:

XYZ Consultants
123 Main Street, #111
Seattle, WA 98101

A PO Box at a USPS post office can only be used to receive regular US mail. Private mailbox services offer the added advantage of allowing you to receive packages from all delivery services, including UPS, FedEx, and private couriers. Many private mailbox services are also capable of phoning you or emailing you when mail or a package arrives. Many are also capable of forwarding your mail and packages to another address.

Some consultants located in a small town or rural area may prefer to use a mailing address in a major city thinking that it will provide them with a marketing advantage. Using a private mailbox service that can forward mail is especially advantageous in these circumstances.

Telephone Service

Your consulting practice should have its own dedicated business telephone number. The use of a home telephone for business is not recommended.

One option is to order a dedicated business telephone service for your office from your telephone or cable company. This option provides the best voice quality and also allows you to easily connect a variety of equipment (such as headsets or digital recorders) to your telephone line.

The second option is to get a dedicated cellular telephone to use as your business telephone. When using a cell phone as your business line, be sure that it provides acceptable voice quality. While call quality may be fine for one-on-one conversations, it can sometimes be difficult to hear people when using a cell phone to participate in a conference call.

The third option is to use a virtual telephone service, such as Google Voice or One Box. These services provide you with a telephone number that connects to a computer server at a central location. When a call is received, it is immediately forwarded to another number. The number that the call is forwarded to is determined by a schedule that you establish within the system.

For example, the virtual telephone service could be programmed to call your office during the day, and your home during the evening. If you are unable to answer the phone at either location, the caller is forwarded to voice mail. A voice mail message is then sent to you by email.

The virtual telephone service is capable of using either a telephone number that is local to your area, or a toll-free telephone number. The cost of the virtual telephone service is very reasonable, often less than the cost of installing an additional telephone line.

Internet Service

High-speed internet service will be needed in your office. If you are renting an office suite, chances are good that acceptable internet services will already be available at your location. If you are operating your office out of your home, your existing home internet service may or may not be acceptable for business use.

For most security management and forensic consultants, an internet service that provides 15 to 25 Mbps download speed and 3 to 5 Mbps upload speed is probably acceptable. Technical security consultants who have a frequent need to upload larger files will probably want a faster internet connection.

It is recommended that you check with your local cable and telephone provider to see what internet service options are available.

Email Address

All independent security consultants should have a dedicated email address that is used in conjunction with their consulting practice. The use of personal or home email addresses for business is not recommended.

I strongly recommend that all consultants use an email address that includes their own internet domain name, such as "bob@ xyzconsultants.com". (See Establishing an Internet Domain above).

I feel that the use of an email address that includes the name of your internet provider (bob@comcast.net) or one of the free email services (bob@gmail.com) presents an image that is less than professional and raises questions as to just how serious you are about your consulting practice.

Stationery

While more and more correspondence is being sent electronically, most independent security consultants will continue to use preprinted stationery of some type. This stationery is typically imprinted with company name, logo, address and telephone number. Website and email addresses may also be imprinted on stationery. The types of stationery commonly used include business cards, letterheads, envelopes, and mailing labels. Some consultants also have preprinted front and back covers that they use for their reports.

It is recommended that all stationery be of a high quality, similar to the type used by attorneys, accountants, and other professionals. Your stationery should use fonts, colors and logos consistent with your visual image (See Establishing Your Visual Image above.)

Some consultants order preprinted business cards, but forgo purchasing letterhead, envelopes, mailing labels, and report covers. Instead, they create various templates within their word processing software that include their company information and logo. A separate template is usually created for letterhead, envelope, mailing label, etc. When drafting a document, the appropriate template is used, and the completed document is then printed on plain paper or exported as a PDF file that can be sent as an email attachment.

Some consultants choose to print a "QR Code" on their business card or other stationery. This allows people who have a QR reading application on their smartphone to scan the card and be immediately directed to the consultant's website. QR codes can also be used to scan contact information such as name, phone number, and email address.

Brochures

It was considered standard practice for many years for an independent security consultant to have a fancy, preprinted brochure. This brochure would explain the services offered by the consultant, their qualifications and experience, and perhaps include references to projects completed by the consultant. This brochure was often a full-color multi-page document that included photos and was printed on glossy heavy-weight paper stock. Brochures of this type could cost up to several dollars each, especially when printed in smaller quantities.

Unfortunately, the information contained in printed brochures can quickly become outdated. Because the cost of printing brochures is so high, most consultants don't update them frequently. As a result, brochures with out-of-date information are used, or the consultant stops using them entirely. A common sight in consultant's offices are stacks of boxes of outdated, unused brochures.

Some consultants today think that the concept of using a printed brochure is entirely obsolete, and instead prefer to communicate using electronic means rather than printed materials. These consultants consider their website to be their "brochure".

Other consultants continue to use printed materials but choose to use something less expensive than the professionally printed, glossy brochure that was used in the past. These consultants often choose to design their own brochures using word processing or desktop publishing software, and then print them using a standard office printer. One popular format used is the "trifold" brochure, where information is printed on an 8 ½" x 11" sheet of paper which is then folded into thirds to create a brochure. The trifold brochure can be easily fit in a standard #10 business envelope and is frequently used in direct mail campaigns.

While self-printed brochures are less impressive than glossy brochures, they offer the advantage of being quickly updated when information changes. The brochures can also be customized before being sent to prospective clients – for example, a brochure being sent to a hospital can emphasize your hospital experience, a brochure being sent to a school can emphasize your school experience, etc.

Consultant Tools

There are various special tools and equipment that the independent security consultant may need depending on their area of practice. Some commonly used items include:

Laptop Computer

Many independent security consultants spend a great deal of time travelling and working at client locations. It is invaluable to have a laptop computer to allow you to work when you are out of your office.

Some consultants choose to use their laptop as their primary computer and use it both in their office and when on the road. Others choose to have a desktop computer in their office and use a separate laptop computer when they are travelling.

There are a number of cloud-based storage services such as Dropbox and Google Drive that automatically synchronize files between two or more computers. Consultants that have both a laptop computer and a desktop computer often use one of these services to avoid having to manually transfer files between computers.

Some consultants who have security concerns about using cloud-based services may choose to use a peer-to-peer file synchronization program.

Digital Camera

Digital cameras are used to take photos for reference purposes and for inclusion in your reports. I actually suggest the use of two cameras: an inexpensive one that you can carry with you at all times and not worry about getting wet or dirty, and a higher-quality camera that you can use to take special photos where you need to use an extended zoom lens or when obtaining an extra high-quality photo is important.

One or more high-capacity memory cards should be provided for each camera. Extra camera batteries should also be provided.

Camcorder

Camcorders are used to create full-motion video recordings. When conducting a security assessment, I find it helpful to do a complete walk around of the site with my camcorder running. This allows me to go back and "virtually" revisit the site, which can be extremely valuable, especially when the project is located hundreds of miles away.

Some consultants also use camcorders to record meetings and to create presentations and training videos.

Digital Voice Recorder

Digital voice recorders are used to record meetings, interview sessions, and telephone calls. When doing a security assessment, I try to record all of my interview sessions. Before writing my report, I will typically go back and listen to my recordings to make sure that I have correctly gathered all information.

A method should be provided to allow you to record telephone calls. This can be done several ways depending on the type of phone you are using.

If using a landline phone, there are adapters that can be connected between the telephone line and your digital voice recorder.

If you are using a cellphone, you can simply place your phone on the desk, put it in speakerphone mode, and turn on your recorder. If you prefer not to use speakerphone mode, there are special earpiece microphones that can be connected to your voice recorder. These are placed between your ear and the phone when you are having a conversation. There are also smartphone apps that allow calls to be recorded.

Be sure to get permission from all parties involved prior to recording their conversations. When using my recorder, I always start the recorder and make an announcement "*If there are no objections, I will be recording this meeting to be sure that I have accurately captured all information...*". I rarely get an objection, and I have a recorded confirmation that I announced that the conversation was being recorded.

Light Meter

Light meters are used to check lighting levels when conducting security assessments or when designing video surveillance systems in outdoor areas. Once quite expensive, light meters are now available at a much lower cost, some for well under $100.

The light meter that you choose should allow display of light levels in both foot-candles and lux. The light meter should have multiple ranges and allow the reading of light levels as low as .1 lux. The light meter should have the ability to accurately measure all types of visible light, including that produced by LED light fixtures. It is recommended that the light meter have a backlighted display that can be read in the dark.

Some light meters are available that are calibrated to National Institute of Standards and Technology (NIST) standards and include a certificate to prove it. This type of certification is not required for most general security consulting work but may be needed for certain forensic cases where the accuracy of light readings might be challenged by the opposing counsel.

It is recommended that your light meter allow the use of a standard photographic tripod, and that a tripod be purchased for use when taking light readings. I have found that taking light readings with a tripod is much easier, particularly when working alone.

Measuring Devices

When making a site survey for a security assessment or a security design project, there is often a need to take accurate measurements of distances. It is recommended that the consultant's toolkit include a 25' tape measure, 100' tape measure, and a 1,000' measuring wheel.

I also use an electronic tape measure, which can make taking accurate measurements much easier in many situations. However, I have found that this tool doesn't work well in every case, particularly when taking measurements outdoors in bright light, requiring me to revert to using a standard tape measure.

LCD Projector

Consultants who frequently do presentations or who conduct training sessions may wish to have their own LCD projector. While projectors are often available in a client's meeting room, there can be a great advantage in using a projector that you are familiar with and that you know for sure works with your computer.

Smartphones can be used as a substitute for many of the individual tools mentioned above. For example, most smartphones now include a camera that can take good quality pictures and videos, and most phones have an app that allows them to make audio recordings. There are even apps that allow you to use your smartphone as a light meter.

I personally use a combination of both my smartphone and other devices in my work. For example, I prefer to use a separate camera for most of my still pictures but use my phone to take videos in place of the camcorder that I previously used. I also continue to use a separate digital audio recorder and light meter. You may find that just a smartphone meets all of your needs just fine.

Chapter 5 - The Security Consultant's Website

Having an effective website is essential for the independent security consultant. Many consultants obtain as much as 80% of their new business as a direct result of their website. Even if a potential client hears about you in another way, they will almost always visit your website first to check you out before they call you.

Not having a website or having a website that displays the words "*Under Construction*", can raise a red flag to potential clients and cause you to be compared unfavorably to those consultants who do have an effective website.

I have a very effective website that generates lots of leads from across the country. Many of my colleagues are dumbfounded when I send them a lead from a prospective client in their own city, asking "*What made them contact you in Seattle when I'm right here in Boston, just ten miles away from their facility?*" The answer is usually because they don't have a very effective website.

Too many websites focus more on being visually impressive than on being effective tools for selling consulting services. Many website designers prioritize style over substance. Here are some suggestions for an effective website based on my personal experience:

- Content is king. Provide as much useful content within your website as you can. Technical tips, articles, and links to other resources are all ways to provide content that is useful to consumers visiting your website. A website may be beautiful to look at, but unless it has great content, it is useless to a potential client. Having a lot of high-quality content on your website can also significantly increase the chances of your site being found by search engines.

- The homepage of your website should provide a complete snapshot of you and the core services that you offer, as well as provide a quick way to contact you. It should not be necessary to click through several pages to find this information – many visitors will never get beyond the home page.

- Most clients will search the internet using specific keywords such as "hospital security consultants" or "apartment security experts" and will often add a reference to the city or state that they are located in, such as "hospital security consultants in Baltimore" or "apartment security experts in Virginia". To increase the chances of your site being found:
    - Show that you are a specialist in your chosen security consulting practice area. Keep your list of service offerings short, preferably ten or less. Don't try to be everything to everyone.
    - If you intend to primarily serve a specific geographic region, clearly state that on your website and provide a listing of the specific cities and states in which you plan to work.
- Your website should focus on the user's problems and how you are uniquely qualified to solve them. Too many security consultant websites shout "Me-Me-Me" and do nothing to speak to the needs of the client. While your website should include a section that briefly describes your background and experience, this is not the place to tell your life story.
- Claims that simply express experience and education are meaningless unless you can specifically translate to the client how they can be of benefit to them. Don't make statements about your credentials without explaining in simple language how they will help the client to solve their specific problems,
- Provide success stories about work that you have done for other clients in the past and the benefits that it has provided. Here are a few examples:
    - *"Helped reduce theft and vandalism at a San Diego mini-storage facility by 33%", decreasing losses and increasing renter satisfaction.*

  - *Allowed the number of security officers required at a Baltimore medical center to be cut in half due to the effective use of security technology".*
  - *Assisted electronics manufacturer in Cleveland to comply with all government security requirements in less than 90 days, allowing them to receive lucrative military contracts.*

- Include testimonials from other clients that you have worked with in the past.
- Describe what makes you different from your competitors in terms of skill and project approach. Don't make empty statements – back them up with facts.
- Use simple non-technical language. Avoid using industry jargon and abbreviations that the average person is unlikely to know.
- Take a look at other security consultant's websites to see what you like and don't like. You should never directly copy another consultant's site but can often get good ideas by looking at what others have done.
- Your website design should use fonts, colors and logos consistent with your visual image (See Establishing Your Visual Image above.)
- Include a "call to action" on every page of your website. Make it easy for a potential client to contact you.
- Update the content frequently on your website to keep it fresh. Sites that have stale content can be ranked poorly by search engines. Make sure that any links and references provided are still current. If you have a "What's New" section on your site, be sure that the most recent article posted is not three years old.

- It is estimated that over 60% of people now browse the web using their smartphone rather than a personal computer or tablet. Be sure that your website is "mobile-friendly" and optimized to support the use of smartphones.
- Provide your telephone number and email address on every page of your website. While your site should have a contact form, it should not be the only way that clients can contact you.
- Providing your address on your website lets people know where you are physically located and can increase your credibility and be reassuring to some clients. A physical street address is best, but a mailing address is better than nothing.

When creating a website, the preferred approach is to retain the services of a professional website developer. The developer should have previous experience in developing websites for professional services firms. Work closely with the developer as the site is being created to make sure that your expectations are being met and that the suggestions listed above are being followed.

The photos, graphical elements, and written content used in your website should be created by you or the developer and not copied from websites or other sources without permission.

If you can't afford to hire a professional developer and feel that you have the ability to learn how to create your own site, there are now a number of services such as Weebly, Wix, and WordPress that allow people without programming skills to develop their own websites. In addition to costing less, these services allow you to make frequent updates and changes to your site without needing to pay a developer to do it.

New consultants may need to get started by building a modest website at the start and then gradually upgrading it as their practice grows. It is better to have an operational website today that is less than perfect than it is to have a dream website that never gets built.

Many clients who call in an independent security consultant know that they have a security problem and need help, but don't know exactly what services that they should buy. Along the same lines, many new security consultants know that they have extensive security skills and want to help clients, but don't know exactly what services to sell.

To help both buyers and sellers, security consulting services must be packaged into service offerings that can be easily described and are well-understood by both parties. Each service offered is intended to solve one or more of a client's specific security problems.

It is usually up to the consultant, not the client, to figure out what is needed and how it should be delivered. A mistake often made by beginning consultants is to simply ask the client *"what do you want me to do?"*. In many cases, the client has a problem but has little or no idea of how to solve it. It is the consultant's role to listen to the client's problem and then come up with the services that the consultant can provide to address the client's needs.

The following are some security consulting service offerings that are commonly needed by clients. Some of these service offerings are of a type that would be provided by security management consultants, others are of a type that would be provided by technical security consultants, and some are of a type that could be provided by either.

Assessments

Conducting assessments is one of the most popular service offerings provided by independent security consultants. When conducting an assessment, the consultant not only provides security expertise, but also gives the client a fresh, unbiased opinion regarding conditions at the client's facilities.

Security management consultants conduct security assessments, which provide an overall appraisal of the client's present security conditions and offer suggestions on ways that security can be improved. These assessments are known by many names, including Security Surveys, Security Audits, Risk Analysis, Threat Assessments, Threat and Vulnerability Assessments, Risk Assessments, Security Gap Analysis, and many others. Most assessments include:

- Identification of the client's security risks, threats, and vulnerabilities.
- Examination of the client's existing security program, including security systems, processes, and procedures.
- Providing a professional opinion as to the adequacy of the client's existing program.
- Identifying security weaknesses and developing specific recommendations for security improvements.

In most cases, the security assessment will be comprehensive and examine every aspect of the client's security program. In some cases, the client may ask that the assessment focus only on a specific topic, such as an assessment of the effectiveness of the client's contract security guard force.

Technical security consultants conduct assessments of the client's existing physical and electronic security systems. This can be a comprehensive assessment of all systems, or just focus on a single type of system, such as the video surveillance system.

Security Planning

Security management consultants help clients to develop long-term plans for their overall security program. Technical security consultants help clients to develop a long-term roadmap for their physical and electronic security systems.

Many regulated industries, such as the cannabis industry, require that a detailed security plan be submitted to a regulatory agency for approval before a business can operate. In many cases, the client needs the help of an independent security consultant to create this plan.

Policies and Procedures Development

Security management consultants help clients to develop written security policies and procedures. This activity typically involves reviewing existing security policies and procedures documents, conducting workshops with client representatives, and the writing of new policies and procedures.

Technical security consultants help clients to develop written security policies and procedures concerning the operation and maintenance of their physical and electronic security systems.

It is important to note that the consultant's role is as much to help the client facilitate the policies and procedures development process as it is to provide security expertise. Often times, the services of an outside consultant are needed to help the client focus on the issues and to make the tough decisions necessary to create effective policies and procedures.

Training

Security management consultants develop training programs and conduct training on a wide variety of topics, including employee security awareness, workplace violence prevention, security management, disaster recovery planning, travel security, and many others.

Technical security consultants develop training programs and conduct training on security system administration, system operation, and system maintenance. Technical security consultants also provide training to facilities personnel to allow them to do in-house installation work and perform maintenance on security systems.

Specification and RFP Development

Security management consultants help clients to write specifications and develop request-for-proposals (RFPs) for guard services and other types of security products and services. Technical security consultants help clients to write specifications and develop RFPs for electronic security systems and other types of physical security devices.

Proposal Review and Contract Negotiation

Independent security consultants assist clients to review proposals received from suppliers of security products and services and help the client to select vendors and negotiate contracts on their behalf.

For security management consultants, this most often involves the review of proposals for guard services and other types of security products and services. For technical security consultants, this usually involves the review of proposals for electronic security systems and other physical security devices.

Design Standards Development

Clients who operate large numbers of facilities nationally or internationally often create written standards to assure that all facilities are designed consistently. These standards are used by architects, engineers, and contractors during the design and construction process.

Independent security consultants assist clients in the development of design standards for security-related elements of the facility. This can include standards for site and building layout, landscaping, lighting, signage, lock hardware, safes and vaults, electronic security systems, and many other items.

Security Design

Independent security consultants assist architects, engineers and clients to incorporate the design of security into new buildings and other facilities.

Security management consultants can provide guidance on general site and building layout, the location of building entrances, lobby and screening station layout, control room design, and other general building design features.

Technical security consultants provide detailed design of electronic security systems and coordinate security system requirements with other members of the design team.

Design Review

Independent security consultants conduct reviews of architectural and engineering drawings prepared by others to assure that security requirements have been properly incorporated into the design of a building. Design reviews may be conducted at the request of the designer for quality control purposes or may be requested by the client or an outside party such as an insurance company or regulatory agency.

Cost Estimating and Budget Development

Security management consultants assist clients in developing and justifying operating budgets for security departments. Security management consultants also help clients to identify ways in which security operating costs can be reduced. Technical security consultants provide detailed cost estimates for security system improvements and help the client to prepare budgets for security system installation and maintenance.

Organizational Review and Planning

Security management consultants conduct reviews of the client's overall security organizational structure and suggest ways in which the organization can be streamlined or made more efficient. Security management consultants also conduct studies that compare the use of outsourced service providers versus the use of in-house personnel.

Recruitment and Selection of Personnel

Security management consultants assist clients to develop job descriptions for security-related positions and help with the interviewing, evaluation, and selection of security personnel.

Project and Event Management

Security management consultants are hired by clients to serve as project managers for the start-up of the security operations at new facilities, and to manage security at special events. Technical security consultants are hired to manage major security upgrade projects and to assist with the start-up of new security systems.

On-Call Security Director

Smaller companies without a security department hire security management consultants to provide "on-call" security director services, sometimes called Security Director as a Service (SDaaS). These services may include managing investigations, providing training, developing policies and procedures, and other activities traditionally performed by an in-house security manager or director.

Forensic Security Consulting

Forensic security consulting services are provided to attorneys and may include reviewing evidence, conducting site surveys, performing threat and risk assessments, providing analysis and expert opinions, writing reports, and testifying at depositions and in court.

Chapter 7 - Determining What and How to Charge

One of the most common questions asked by beginning independent security consultants is "What should I charge?" Within this chapter, I will answer this question and explain the processes used to establish your fees, charge for your expenses, and collect what is owed to you.

Establishing Your Hourly Billing Rate

The independent security consultant needs to understand that they are operating a business, not just working as a contract or temporary employee. As a business, you need to charge enough to pay yourself a competitive salary, provide yourself with benefits, cover all of your expenses, and earn a reasonable profit as a business owner

The first thing to do when determining what to charge is to establish your hourly billing rate. Even if you charge by the day or charge a fixed-fee amount for your services, your hourly rate is the building block used to establish your prices.

To determine your hourly billing rate, you should take the following steps:

<u>Step #1 – Determine Annual Labor Cost</u>

The Annual Labor Cost is what it costs the consulting firm to employ the consultant performing the consulting work on an annual basis. This includes salary, payroll taxes, the employer's share of Social Security and Medicare, and the cost of any benefits (such as medical insurance) provided by the employer.

Your Annual Labor Cost includes the following:

- Annual gross salary that you expect to earn. This would typically be similar to what you were being paid at your last job, or what you could reasonably expect to earn if you went to work at another employer. For the sake of this example, let's assume that your salary is $150,000 annually.
- One-half of Social Security and Medicare. When you are working as an employee, one-half of your Social Security and Medicare is paid by your employer. Now that you are

self-employed, the one-half that was previously paid by your employer must be paid by you and should be considered part of your direct labor costs. Currently, the combined rate for Social Security and Medicare is 15.3%, so one-half of this amount is 7.65%.

- Annual employee benefits. This would be the cost of any employee benefits, such as health insurance, that you provide to yourself as an "employee" of your consulting practice. For the sake of this example, we will assume that $25,000 in annual benefits are provided.

So, to calculate the Annual Labor Cost using our examples, we would total up the following figures:

Annual Gross Salary:	$150,000
One-half of Social Security and Medicare (Annual Salary x 7.65%):	$11,475
Annual Employee Benefits:	$25,000
Total Annual Labor Costs	**$186,475**

Total Annual Labor Costs

Step #2 – Determine Your Annual Overhead Costs

Your Annual Overhead is the annual cost of operating your consulting practice in addition to your salary. Overhead typically includes things such as rent, telephone and internet service, insurance, office supplies, business taxes and other expense items

Overhead costs should only include expenses that are not directly attributable to any specific project or client. For example, if you paid for travel to attend a conference for continuing education, the cost of this would be part of your overhead. However, if you travelled out of town to work on a specific client's project, the cost of this would not be part of your overhead but would instead be a Direct Expense. I will talk more about Direct Expenses later.

Here is an example of what a list of Annual Overhead costs might look like for a consultant who operates out of their home:

Advertising & Marketing	$4,000
Business Licenses	$300
Computer & Internet	$2,000
Continuing Education	$2,000
Professional Fees	$800
Insurance	$4,500
Office Supplies	$900
PO Box Rent	$300
Publications	$600
Software	$700
Taxes	$3,700
Telephone	$2,200
Tools & Equipment	$2,000
Travel, non-billable	$12,000
Total Annual Overhead Cost	**$36,000**

Total Annual Overhead Costs

Step #3 – Determine Your Total Annual Costs

Your Total Annual Labor Costs and Your Total Annual Overhead Costs are added together to determine your Total Annual Costs.

Total Annual Labor Costs:	$186,475
Total Annual Overhead Costs:	$36,000
Total Annual Costs	**$222,475**

Total Annual Costs

Step #4 – Determine Your Targeted Revenue

As a business owner, you are entitled to receive compensation for your capital investment in the business (the money that you invested to open your practice) and the risks that you are taking as a business owner. Many independent consultants fail to consider that they are both a business owner and an "employee" of their consulting practice – and need to get separately compensated for each.

Targeted Revenue is the total amount of money that you need to take in to pay your salary and expenses plus earn a profit to compensate you for your investment and risk. Targeted Total Revenue is calculated by adding a Gross Profit Margin to your Total Annual Costs.

Gross Profit Margin is calculated as a percentage of your Total Annual Costs. The Gross Profit Margin charged by most larger consulting firms typically ranges between 30% and 50%. For smaller firms, this rate is usually between 25% and 30%. For this example, we will use a Gross Profit Margin of 25%.

Here is the formula to calculate your Target Revenue:

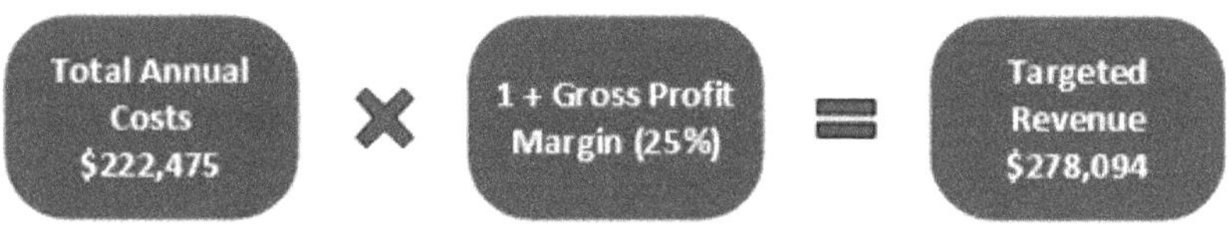

Targeted Revenue

Step #5 - Determine Total Available Hours

Total Available Hours are the total hours that the consultant is available to work during the year. The number used as the baseline for most calculations is 2,080 hours (40 hours x 52 weeks), but this figure does not factor in holidays or a vacation. A more realistic baseline is 1,920 hours, which allows ten days for holidays as well as two weeks for vacation.

Individual consultants may choose to use a higher or lower figure in their calculations, but for the sake of our example, we will use 1,920 as our Total Available Hours figure.

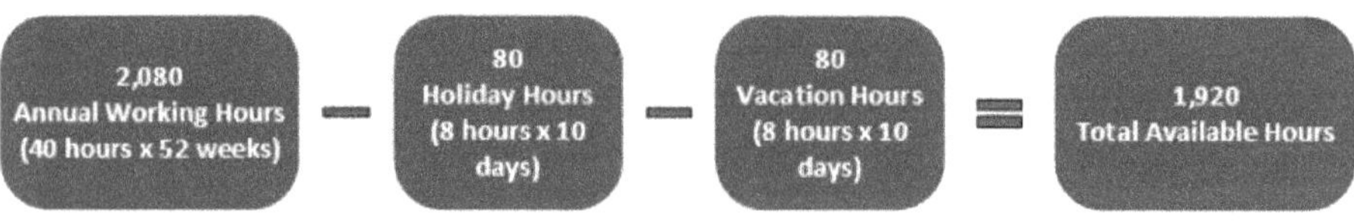

Total Available Hours

Step #6 – Determine Your Utilization Rate

Not all Total Available Hours are billable to clients. The independent security consultant must spend time selling their services, managing the business, and performing a multitude of other activities that cannot be billed to clients. There may also be slow periods throughout the year, where despite your best efforts, there are no projects to work on and therefore no client that you can charge your time to.

The ratio between billable time and Total Available Hours is known as the Utilization Rate and is calculated as a percentage. For example, if there were 2,000 Total Available Hours in a year, and you managed to bill for only 1,000 hours, your Utilization Rate would be 50% (1000/2000). A consultant who had the same number of Total Available Hours but managed to bill 1,600 hours would have a Utilization Rate of 80% (1600/2000).

Utilization Rate

Your Utilization Rate is determined by a number of factors, including the type of work that you do, how effective you are at selling your services, how well you manage your time, and how long you have been in business.

Technical security consultants tend to have the highest Utilization Rates because they often get large projects that allow them to bill for their time continuously for weeks and even months.

On the other hand, certain forensic security consultants may find that their specialized expertise is needed only a limited number of times per year, and even when retained, find their engagements to be of a relatively short duration. As a result, they may have a much lower Utilization Rate.

The Utilization Rate for most security management consultants typically falls in between these two extremes. Security management consultants who do a good job of selling their services can stay busy throughout much of the year, but there may still be slow periods where there is no work.

It is difficult for a new consultant to accurately determine their Utilization Rate when first establishing their practice. To get started, it is suggested that you use a 50% Utilization Rate in your calculations. Your actual Utilization Rate will probably be lower during your first year, but this will give you a starting point. As your practice becomes better established, your Utilization Rate will increase. Well-established independent security consultants can have a Utilization Rate of 85% or higher.

Effectively managing your utilization rate is one of the biggest factors in determining how profitable your consulting practice will be. One major cause of low utilization rates is a lack of paid projects to work on, which is one of the reasons that so much emphasis is placed on sales and marketing in later chapters of this book.

Step #7 – Determine Your Total Billable Hours

Your Total Billable Hours are the total hours that you can expect to bill clients on an annual basis. Total Billable Hours are determined by multiplying Total Available Hours times the Utilization Rate. For the purposes of this example, we will use 50% as our Utilization Rate.

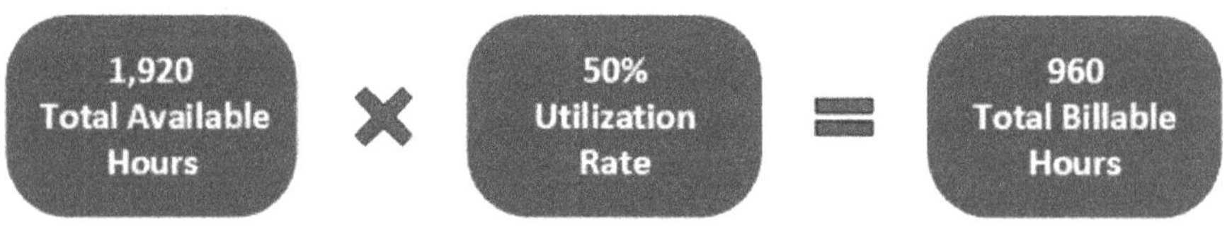

Total Billable Hours

Step #8 – Calculate Your Hourly Rate

Your Hourly Rate is calculated by dividing your Targeted Revenue by your total Billable Hours.

Hourly Rate

It is customary for consultants to round this number off to an even figure, so would probably use $290 per hour or $300 per hour as their hourly billing rate.

Charging for Your Services

Once you have established your hourly rate, you need to determine how you intend to charge your clients for your services. There are five methods used by independent security consultants to charge for their services:

Straight Hourly

Straight hourly is the simplest way to charge for your services. The client tells you what they want, and you quote your hourly rate. You do what's needed and send them an invoice for your total hours.

This method is commonly used when you have worked previously with a client and established a level of trust. This method is seldom used with new clients because they would likely be uncomfortable with the open-ended nature of the arrangement.

Straight Hourly with Estimate

When this method is used, the client calls you in and tells you what they want done. You prepare an estimate of the total number of hours that you think the job will take and tell the client your hourly billing rate and the estimated number of hours.

You keep track of the actual hours that you spend on the job, and bill the client for your total time, which may be more or less than your original estimate. If you intend to charge more than your estimate, it is considered a courtesy to get your client's permission before going over the originally estimated amount.

This method is commonly used when the scope of work is not well-defined and when it may be difficult to determine the exact amount of work required in advance.

Straight Hourly with Not-to-Exceed Amount

When this method is used, the client calls you in and tells you what they want done. You determine the maximum number of hours that you think the job will take and multiply this by your hourly rate to get a "not-to-exceed" cost. You guarantee that the total charges will not exceed this amount.

You keep track of the actual hours that you spend on the job. If the actual hours are less than your estimate, the client pays only for the actual hours. If the actual hours are greater than your estimate, the client pays only the estimated amount – you don't get paid for the excess hours.

Clients love this method because it is a "win-win" for them: if the work takes less time than estimated, they reap the savings. If the work takes longer than estimated, you absorb the loss.

I personally dislike this method because I feel that it places the risk on the consultant for cost overruns, without offering any corresponding opportunity for reward if the project comes in under budget.

I have also seen much dishonesty around this billing method at some consulting firms – the total number of hours billed seems to miraculously come in at or just under the total estimated amount, even if the actual number of hours worked were considerably less.

This practice is particularly prevalent in some larger consulting firms, where overbilling to get every dollar out of a contract seems to be accepted with a wink and a nod.

Fixed-Fee Amount

When this method is used, the client calls you in and tells you what they want done. You then prepare a proposal defining the scope of work and offer to perform the work for a fixed-fee amount. The client is billed a fixed-fee amount regardless of the amount of time the work actually takes. If the project takes less time than expected, the consultant benefits, but if the project takes more time than expected, the consultant absorbs the loss.

The fixed-fee method of billing is sometimes also known as "flat-rate" billing or "lump-sum" billing. Many clients like fixed-fee billing because they know in advance exactly what they will be paying.

Many consultants hesitate to use the fixed-fee method because they are afraid of cost overruns, but by playing it safe, are denying themselves the potential upside when a project can be completed under budget.

I personally prefer the fixed-fee billing arrangement and try to use it on every consulting project I can.

Retainer Fee Agreements

Some clients want to have a security consultant "on-call" at all times and are willing to pay a monthly fee to make this possible.

For example, many security consultants now offer what is known as "Security Director as a Service" (SDaaS) to smaller organizations who don't have a security director on staff but still need someone to handle security issues when they arise.

To obtain this service, the client agrees to pay the consultant a fixed amount each month and is guaranteed a certain amount of the consultant's time. For example, a client might pay the consultant a monthly fee of $4,000. This fee would guarantee up to ten hours of the consultant's time each month.

As the month goes on, the client calls in the consultant when needed, and the consultant keeps track of the time. If the total time is less than ten hours, the client pays no additional charge, but if the time exceeds ten hours, the client pays for the additional hours at the consultant's hourly rate.

Some retainer agreements allow the client who doesn't use all hours during the month to roll them over to the next month, while other agreements state that the client loses any hours that they don't use during a specific month.

Travel Time

Travel time is the time that you spend traveling to and from your office and the location of the client's project. In the case of an in-town project, travel time could be the half-hour that it takes you to drive to the client's office from your home office. In the case of an out-of-town project, travel time could be measured in many hours or even days.

Different consultants have different policies regarding travel time. Some consultants consider travel time to be fully billable and include travel time in their estimates for hourly and fixed-fee projects. Other consultants consider travel time to be part of their overhead and don't charge for it at all. Still others have a policy that falls in between these two extremes, and only charge the client for a portion of their travel time or bill the client for travel time at a reduced rate.

The bottom line is that, as a self-employed consultant you have to be compensated for travel time somehow. Whether this is in the form of an hourly charge to the client for your time, or an increased hourly rate to compensate for your overhead is up to you. The important thing is to clearly communicate how travel time is handled in your proposals and contracts so that there are no surprises for the client.

Charging for Expenses

The independent security consultant often incurs expenses when working on a client's project. This commonly occurs when the consultant travels out of town to work on a project, incurring expenses for airfare, hotel, rental car, and other such items.

Other expenses incurred on behalf of the client can include the cost of printing and binding reports, the cost of research or crime forecasting services, the cost of printing drawings, and many other items.

When expenses are incurred as the result of a specific project or client, they are considered "Direct Expenses". It is a standard practice within the consulting profession to ask clients to reimburse the consultant for all Direct Expenses in addition to the amount that they are paying for consulting services. For this reason, Direct Expenses are also called "Reimbursable Expenses".

When a proposal is submitted for consulting services, the proposal will specify the cost of consultant services using one of the five billing methods described above, and then usually specify that the client will reimburse the consultant for expenses in addition to this amount. For example, a proposal might specify that "*Security Assessment will be provided at the rate of $300 per hour, for an amount not-to-exceed $9,000, plus reimbursable expenses.*" In some cases, the consultant might include a rough estimate of expenses so that the client is not surprised when the bill comes.

Many large companies and government agencies have strict guidelines on reimbursing expenses to their employees, and usually expect any consultant that they hire to follow these same guidelines. These guidelines usually place limits on the amounts that will be reimbursed for airfare, hotel, rental cars, and meals. When working with a client that has travel guidelines, the consultant should know this in advance.

To obtain reimbursement of expenses, many clients require meticulous accounting of all items along with copies of receipts. Some clients may request the original receipt rather than just a copy.

Most consultants charge the client for only the actual amount of expenses incurred. Some larger consulting firms may tack on an "administrative fee" to reimburse themselves for the costs they incur when processing these expenses.

In the beginning years of my consulting practice, I charged separately for expenses just like most other consultants do. I now prefer to include all reimbursable expenses into my fixed-fee proposals. When preparing a proposal, I estimate travel costs and all other expenses and add them to my consulting fees to establish a fixed fee cost. The client knows the total cost of the project in advance and the billing process is greatly simplified. I have been burned a few times when travel expenses ended up being greater than expected (such as a surprise increase in airfare) but have also benefited when expenses turned out to be less than expected.

Charging for Use of a Vehicle

Consultants who use their personal vehicle for project-related travel have the option of charging a "mileage rate" to get compensated for the expense of operating their vehicle. The Standard Mileage Rate published by the Internal Revenue Service (IRS) is most commonly used. This rate is updated every year. As of the date of this writing, the rate is 67 cents per mile.

Some consultants charge their clients for every mile driven; some charge only for mileage that exceeds a certain minimum distance (say 50 miles) from their office location. Still others don't charge their clients for mileage at all.

Regardless of whether or not you choose to charge your clients for mileage, you should keep track of all miles driven for business purposes. Business-related mileage that is not reimbursed by clients is considered to be an overhead expense and should be tracked in your accounting system. The IRS has different methods in which vehicle-related expenses can be deducted and specific rules on what records must be kept in order to claim these deductions. Consult with your accounting advisor to determine which method is best for you.

Tracking Time and Expenses

It is important that the independent security consultant keeps track of time and reimbursable expenses accurately. This makes billing the client easier and provides you with backup documentation should a client ever question an invoice.

Many consultants are careless about tracking time and find themselves having to construct a time record from memory when it comes time to bill the client. Along the same lines, many consultants stuff all of their expense receipts in an envelope, and then try to figure out what each receipt was for when it comes time to prepare their bills. In some cases, the consultant will find an expense receipt many months later that they forgot to bill a client for and must either absorb the cost of the expense themself, or embarrassingly go back to the client later to ask for reimbursement.

To avoid these difficulties, it is recommended that the consultant keep track of time and expenses on a daily basis. Yes, I said daily, not weekly or monthly. Take the time to do this religiously as a part of your daily routine.

I recommend that you keep track of time and expenses even when you are doing projects for a fixed fee amount. This allows you to determine the profitability of a project after it is done and gives you the data necessary to more accurately predict costs for future projects.

Time and expenses can be entered into a handwritten log, in a spreadsheet, or directly into your accounting software. There are also numerous smartphone apps that can be used to track time, expenses, and mileage. Most of these apps allow time and expense information to be exported to a spreadsheet, or directly into your accounting software.

Payment Terms

Payment terms specify how and when the consultant will be paid by the client. It is important that payment terms be crystal clear at the start of any client relationship so that there are no surprises.

Many new consultants are hesitant to talk to clients about payment terms, afraid that the client will think that asking about payment at the start of a project may be perceived as a sign of desperation. The truth is that most clients respect the consultant that stands up for their rights during the negotiation process and understand completely when the consultant asks about payment.

The payment terms used by the independent security consultant should be similar to those used by other professionals such as accountants and lawyers. These terms typically call for some type of advance payment at the start of the project, with payment of the remaining balance occurring at the conclusion of the project or shortly thereafter.

It is common for professional service providers to request an advance payment prior to starting work on a project. This advance payment is sometimes called an "advance", a "deposit", or a "retainer" (not to be confused with the Retainer Fee Agreement mentioned above.).

I call these advance payments a "retainer". The purpose of receiving a retainer is threefold:

- It provides immediate cash flow to the consultant, fully or partially offsetting any out-of-pocket expenses that the consultant may incur in performing the project.
- It reduces the risk of non-payment for services by the client.
- It can ensure that the person ordering the work has the authority to do so and that the consultant is already set up as a vendor in the client's accounting system.

The amount of the retainer is typically one-quarter to one-half of the total anticipated consulting fees. I typically ask for a retainer payment of one-third of the total amount. So, for example, on a $9,000 project, I would ask for a $3,000 retainer.

When I first started my consulting practice, I used to be hesitant to ask for a retainer payment, assuming that the client would think I was a small-time operator by needing to ask for money in advance. When I later went to work for the world's largest risk consulting firm, I was surprised to find that they were stricter than I was when it came to requiring a retainer – they would not start work for even a Fortune 100 corporation until a retainer check was in hand.

Some clients have policies that prevent the payment of any amount in advance, including retainer payments. For example, many government agencies are subject to laws that prevent them from making advance payments. In my consulting practice, I am willing to forgo the retainer payment from government agency clients that I otherwise believe will pay me in a timely manner. For most other projects, I almost always insist on a retainer payment.

When the consulting project is completed, the client should be billed for the full amount of consulting fees and expenses, less the retainer amount. The invoice should specify payment terms that state how quickly the invoice must be paid. Some commonly used payment terms include:

Due upon Receipt: The full amount of the invoice is due on the day it is received.

Net 10 Days: The full amount of the invoice is due ten days after it is received.

Net 30 Days: The full amount of the invoice is due thirty days after it is received.

Net 45 Days: The full amount of the invoice is due 45 days after it is received.

2% 10 Days, Net 30: A 2% discount may be taken on the amount of the invoice if it is paid within ten days, otherwise the full amount must be paid within thirty days.

Some consultants offer discounts such as these to encourage fast payment, but unless you have an urgent need for cash, it is usually not worth the cost. (You are paying about a 37% annualized rate of interest to get the money 20 days earlier).

Also, some clients may pay the invoice later than 10 days but still take the discount, putting you in a position of having to go after the improperly deducted amount. Many suppliers don't bother to pursue this, which is why the client tries to get away with it in the first place.

Some private corporations may have policies that prevent retainer payments and/or require that the consultant wait an extended period of time for payment. I submitted a proposal to a large foreign-owned corporation that not only refused to pay a retainer, but also stated that it would be 90 to 120 days before my invoices would be paid. When I objected, they stated that this was their standard policy for all vendors. I decided that this was a company that I didn't want to work for.

Payment terms that specify the amount of retainer payment that you require and how quickly you expect your invoices to be paid should be clearly specified in your proposal and agreed to by your client before you start work.

When working as a subcontractor to an architect, engineer, or other consultant, the "pay when paid" rule usually applies. This usually means that you cannot request a retainer, and when submitting an invoice, you cannot expect payment until the firm hiring you has itself been paid.

For example, if you are a technical security consultant working for an architectural firm, you submit your invoices to the architect. The architect then includes your invoice amount in their firm's next invoice to the client. When the architect gets paid by the client, the architect pays you. It can sometimes take 90 days or more for this process to play out.

It can be even worse when you are working as a subcontractor for another subcontractor who is in turn working for the architect. The consultant at the end of the line can sometimes wait six months or more for payment.

When I was just starting out, I did lots of projects for architects and engineers and played the waiting game just like everyone else. I have waited as long as eleven months to get paid. In my early years, waiting long periods of time to get paid was a real hardship. Now, I can easily afford to wait to get paid, but still prefer to work for clients who pay me promptly.

As a result, I now try to avoid working as a second or third tier subcontractor on projects, preferring instead to work directly for the end-user client. This undoubtedly costs me some opportunities, but at this point in my career, I can afford it. As a beginning security consultant, you may find yourself forced to work on projects where delayed payment is a fact of life. As long as you know this in advance, you can prepare for it.

Submitting Your Invoices

Invoices for projects lasting less than a month are typically invoiced at the end of the project. If the project was performed on an hourly fee plus expenses basis, the client would be billed for the total hours of service provided, plus reimbursable expenses, less the amount of the retainer payment. If the project was performed on a fixed-fee basis, the client would be billed for a fixed-fee amount, plus reimbursable expenses, less the amount of the retainer payment.

If a project extends beyond one month, it is customary to submit invoices on a monthly basis. These are sometimes called "progress" invoices.

When preparing a progress invoice for work being performed on an hourly fee plus expenses basis, the client would be billed for the total hours of service provided during the previous month, plus any reimbursable expenses incurred during that month. If the project extends over several months, the client would be invoiced again in a similar manner each month. When the project is completed, a final invoice would be submitted. Any retainer payment that was received is applied to the last invoice.

If a fixed-fee project extends over several months, the estimated percentage of completion is figured at the end of each month. From this percentage, the amount the consultant is owed is determined and any amounts paid in any previous progress invoices deducted.

For example, let's say a project has a fixed-fee amount of $45,000. At the end of the first month, the project is one-third complete, so the consultant is due $15,000 (one-third of $45,000). A progress invoice for this amount, plus any expenses incurred in the first month is submitted.

At the end of the second month, the project is two-thirds complete, so the consultant is due $30,000 (two-thirds of $45,000), less the $15,000 that was paid for the first month. A progress invoice for this amount, plus any expenses incurred in the second month is submitted. When the project is finally completed, a final invoice would be submitted. Any retainer payment that was received is applied to the last invoice.

Collecting Payment

Collecting payments promptly from clients is essential, particularly when you are just starting out and you need to receive that client's check to pay your bills. Here are a few tips to help you to get paid more promptly:

- Make sure that the clients that you work for are creditworthy. Trust your gut feelings and always ask for a retainer payment when in doubt.
- Never start work until you have a signed proposal or contract, despite pleas from the client that you get started while the paperwork is being processed. If the work is so important that you must start immediately, it should be important enough that the client can find a way to expedite the paperwork.
- Be sure that the person requesting your services has the authority to make purchasing decisions. Sometimes an overzealous employee at a company may ask for services when they have no authority to do so. Asking for a retainer payment in advance is usually one way to make sure that this doesn't happen – checks can't usually be written until the proper authorizations are in place.
- Make sure that you have fully complied with all of the paperwork requirements of the client, including requests to submit a Form W-9 or Certificate of Insurance.
- Be sure to carefully read all of the client's requirements for invoice submission and be sure that you have fully complied with them.
- Before submitting an invoice, particularly to a first-time client, call and ask if they are happy with the work performed. If so, tell the client that you will be submitting your invoice, and ask them to call if there are any issues with it.
- If the client has strict policies on reimbursable expenses, consider submitting two separate invoices: one for your consulting fees, and another one for your expenses. I have seen

$20,000 invoices held up because of a dispute about a $20 expense on a hotel bill.

- If an invoice is more than a few days past due, immediately call your client to find out what's going on. Don't be shy about attempting to collect what's owed to you - you kept your commitment to them; you have a right to insist that they keep their commitment to you.
- Don't start new work for clients who haven't promptly paid past invoices and still owe you money. For ongoing projects, consider pausing work on the project if the client is not paying you according to the agreed upon terms.

Changes in Scope of Work

When performing consulting projects, you will often encounter situations where the services requested by the client change during the course of the project. For example, a technical security consultant may have a signed agreement with a client to design a video surveillance system. During the course of the design process, the client decides that an access control system is also needed and wants to include this in the design.

Along the same lines, a security management consultant may have a contract to conduct a security assessment for a warehouse. When the consultant arrives to perform the site survey, the client points out that they also own an office building across the street that they want included in the assessment.

Changes in the scope of work need to be dealt with as soon as they are discovered. When a client requests something that is in addition to what has already been agreed to, you should tell the client that you would be glad to perform the additional work, and that you will prepare an addendum to the original proposal or contract.

These addendums are sometimes called "change orders" and should clearly specify the nature of the additional work and the additional fee that you will charge. If the additional work will have an impact on the project schedule, you should also specify any additional time that may be required to complete the project.

Addendums should be approved in writing by the client prior to any additional work being done. In a desire to please their client, consultants sometimes jump right in and start performing additional work without requesting additional compensation or getting approval. When going back to the client at the end of the project, they often find it difficult or impossible to get paid for the additional work that they have performed.

The ability to properly manage changes in scope can be a key factor in determining the profitability of your consulting practice.

Requests to Lower Your Prices

The independent security consultant will often get requests to lower their hourly rate, or to reduce the total amount of fixed-fee proposals. This situation is handled differently by different consultants – some are rigid and absolutely refuse to lower their prices – while others are glad to substantially cut their fees in order to win a project. Here are some thoughts on this topic.

- Reductions in prices should only be made when it makes good business sense. For example, if you encounter a potential project that has several hundred hours of billable work, reducing your hourly rate somewhat makes sense because having this volume of work increases your utilization rate, and reduces the sales efforts that would be needed to sell this time to other clients.
- Some large corporations and government agencies have "fee caps" that prevent them paying more than a certain hourly rate for consulting services. For example, a client's purchasing department may have a rule that states that no consultant may be paid more than $300 per hour without special approval. A consultant with a normal billing rate of $350 per hour may find that it makes sense to reduce their hourly rate to $300 so that it falls beneath this fee cap.
- Reductions in fixed-fee proposal amounts should only be made when there is a corresponding reduction in the scope of work. For example, a security management consultant may have submitted a proposal for $10,000 to

conduct four days of training. The client comes back and says that there is only $8,000 in the budget. The consultant might agree to accept the $8,000 but should state that three rather than four days of training will be provided. Agreeing to provide the same scope of work for a lesser fee can send a message that your fees are arbitrary, and the client may always try to negotiate for a lower fee on all projects going forward.

- When a consultant is working as a subcontractor to another consultant, it is customary to agree to work at a lower rate to allow the prime consultant to make a profit on your services. However, care should be taken to make sure that you are still able to make a reasonable profit. Some prime consultants ask their subcontractors to work at unsustainably low rates in order to win contracts. These consultants are in essence asking their subcontractors to subsidize their projects for them.
- Some clients may ask you to work on one project at a greatly reduced price, promising lots of future work at your regular rates. I have found that it almost never happens this way – once you have agreed to work for a lower price on one project, the client will expect the same or even a greater discount on the next project.
- You will occasionally encounter a client that is what I call a "wheeler-dealer". These clients will always try to negotiate a lower price, asking you to lower your hourly rate and arguing that the work won't take you nearly as long as you have estimated. They seem to enjoy haggling over price and often ask you to throw in additional services for free. I have found clients of this type to be nothing but trouble. In addition to asking you to work at a reduced price, they are often difficult and demanding to work for, and slow to pay their bills. I personally choose to avoid this type of client at all costs.

- Just because a company is big and prestigious doesn't mean they are a good client to work for. For example, in my market area, there is one well-known company that frequently hires consultants to do their in-house security design projects. Unfortunately, they always ask their consultants to work at rock-bottom rates – closer to an hourly wage paid to an employee than an hourly fee charged by a consultant. The client is also slow to pay, difficult to work for, and prohibits the consultant from using them as a reference or even mentioning their name in proposals to other clients. Do you need this type of client? I don't.
- Think about the other project opportunities that you may be passing up while you are working on projects at a reduced rate. It makes no sense at all to get tied up on projects that are only marginally profitable when there are plenty of opportunities to work at your regular rates.

Chapter 8 - Selling Security Consulting Services

The ability to effectively sell your security consulting services is crucial to the success of your consulting practice. The inability to obtain a consistent amount of profitable work is the leading cause of failure among security consulting firms.

Basic Axioms

1. In order to succeed at selling your services, you must have a proactive sales program in place. Simply hanging out your shingle and hoping that clients will call you is wishful thinking. A line from a classic movie says, "if you build it, they will come". The truth is, in security consulting, you can build it, but they will <u>not</u> come unless you sell them on doing so.
2. There are no magic bullets when it comes to selling. I get regularly asked by new consultants *"where can I place an advertisement to get work?"*, *"who do you know that can refer clients to me?"* and a multitude of similar questions. Sorry folks, it simply isn't that easy. There is no one single thing that will bring business to you – you must use a combination of different strategies and methods to reach out to potential clients and convince them to hire you.
3. Selling should be an integral part of your daily activities as a security consultant. You should be selling every day, even if you already have plenty of work. Selling should be ingrained in your soul. If you don't want to sell, you should probably think twice about becoming an independent security consultant.
4. Action is key. When selling, any type of selling activity is better than no selling activity at all. The more effective your sales techniques are, the better that you will do, but even techniques that are only marginally effective will work if they are done often enough. You have to repeatedly take actions to sell your services throughout your consulting career in order to succeed.

The Challenges of Selling Security Consulting

One big problem when selling independent security consulting services is that the profession is relatively unknown. Many potential clients are completely unaware of what an independent security consultant does or what services they provide. Clients who have security problems have traditionally relied upon guard companies, alarm companies, locksmiths and private investigators to provide them with security advice. Many of these clients would never even think of calling in an independent security consultant. While there is a better awareness of independent security consultants than when I started in 1985, this still remains a problem.

Because of this, the first challenge in selling security consulting services is to sell the client on the concept of using an independent security consultant in the first place. To sell this concept, you must convince the client of the benefits of using an independent professional instead of one of the traditional providers of security products and services. Only after the consultant has sold the concept can they go about selling themselves.

The second challenge in selling independent security consulting services is that most security projects are event driven – something has to happen in order to motivate the client to initiate the project.

For example, most clients don't think to have a security assessment done until after a major incident has occurred. In the case of a security management consultant, this could be triggered by a recent burglary or a robbery; in the case of a cybersecurity consultant, this could be triggered by a breach of the client's computer system that resulted in the theft of sensitive data.

Along the same lines, the technical security consultant is most often called in when a client is building a new building or replacing their security systems, and the forensic security consultant is usually only called in when an attorney has a case that demands an expert in the area of security.

The underlying fact in all of these examples is that the client must have an immediate need in order for the consultant's services to be relevant – it is unlikely that any amount of selling would be effective if the client didn't have an immediate need.

To be sure, there are exceptions – some well-managed companies may choose to have security assessments or security training done proactively – but in the vast majority of cases, the client will have to have an immediate problem to prompt them to call in a consultant.

In order to effectively sell security consulting services, you have to have the ability to connect with clients that have an immediate need. Since it is highly unlikely that any client that you call will have an immediate need on the day you call them, the challenge is to get them to remember you so that when they <u>do</u> have a need for your services, they will give you a call.

So, in summary, the two major challenges in selling independent security consulting services are: 1) you need to sell the concept of using an independent security consultant before you can sell yourself; and 2) your prospective clients are unlikely to need you when you first contact them – you must get them to remember you when a need arises – perhaps months or years later.

Understand Your Competition

I frequently mentor people who want to become security consultants, many of whom are operating in other cities, but some who are starting practices in my own market area. I sometimes get asked: "Why are you helping people who will become your competitors?"

The truth is, I have no fear at all of competing with other independent security consultants. In fact, I think that the more consultants that there are, the better off all of us will be. Why? Because each new consultant out there is helping to sell the concept of using an independent security consultant, making it better for everyone. I am convinced that once a client is sold on the concept, I have a better than average chance of convincing him to hire me. If the client finds another consultant that they prefer to work with, so be it.

I consider my biggest competition to be the other sources of security advice that a potential client may choose to receive "security consulting" from: guard companies, security equipment vendors, locksmiths, and local police departments who provide free crime prevention advice.

To compete against these other sources of security advice, most of my sales campaigns are directed towards educating clients on the benefit of using independent consultants in general, rather than my consulting firm specifically. This strategy works for me because I have established myself as one of the leading independent security consultants in my region.

I also consider in-house consultants to be a major source of competition. More and more of my larger clients have developed extensive in-house security consulting capabilities. Many large companies who were previously good clients of mine now use my services rarely or not at all.

When I started my consulting practice more than 35 years ago, it was rare to find a large company that had security systems design expertise in-house. Because of this, I was hired to design and specify security systems for some of the largest corporations in the United States. Now it is rare to find a large company that doesn't have one or more in-house security systems experts, greatly reducing the need for them to hire outside consultants.

As a result of these changes, I have shifted the focus of my sales efforts. My sales campaigns now target medium-sized organizations that don't have in-house security capabilities.

As you can see from my examples, competition can come from other sources, not just from other consultants.

The situation can be different in every area of practice and in each geographical market area. For example, there may be one leading consulting firm in your chosen specialty that dominates the market. Competing with this firm is tough because they have an established track record, and clients don't want to risk hiring a young, unproven firm such as your own.

Or you may find that there are numerous qualified consultants in your chosen specialty who are retired, have a good pension, and are working just to keep themselves occupied. You may find that competing with these consultants on the basis of price is impossible.

You may also find that there are other sources of the services that you provide available for free or at little charge. For example, if consulting services on mailroom security are provided by the Postal Service for free, you might face challenges in selling these same services to clients for a fee.

The important thing is to identify all sources of competition, either direct or indirect, and establish a strategy for dealing with this competition head-on. This may involve coming up with a different marketing approach, modifying your service offerings, or going after a completely different type of client.

A big mistake often made by new consultants is to dream up a specific service offering in their head and try to sell it to clients who have no need or desire to buy it. Ultimately, the marketplace, not you, will determine the viability of a specific product or service.

Create a Marketing Database

A marketing database is a tool that allows you to store and manage information about people who can buy your services directly or connect you to other people who can. Your marketing database will become the foundation for all of your marketing efforts, including direct sales calls, mailings, and other promotional activities. Your marketing database should contain information on three types of people:

Prospects

A prospect is a prospective client – someone with whom you would like to do business. Prospects are the actual people to whom you will sell your services.

Influencers

Influencers are people who may not buy your services themselves but can refer you to prospects who can. Influencers can include professional advisors, consultants in related fields, and sellers of security products and services.

Past Clients

Past clients are people that you have provided security consulting services to in the past. Past clients can be both prospects for additional services, and influencers who can refer you to other prospects.

The marketing database that you use should allow you to efficiently manage the large amount of information that you will eventually amass as you build your consulting practice. In the past, people used manual systems (such as 3" x 5" index cards) to manage this type of information. Today, most people use some type of computer database software.

The first option is to use spreadsheet software, such as Microsoft Excel, as your marketing database. Spreadsheets can work well when you are just getting started and have only a limited amount of data but might become cumbersome to use as your database grows.

The second option is to use a relational database program, such as Microsoft Access, as your marketing database. This type of program offers more flexibility and can more efficiently manage large amounts of data. However, creating a marketing database using this type of program requires a certain amount of skill. If you don't have this skill yourself, you will probably need to hire someone to help you.

The third option is to use Customer Relationship Management (CRM) software. This software is specifically designed to manage information regarding your prospects and clients and includes many tools that can make selling easier. Most CRM software used today is cloud-based and is available for a modest monthly subscription fee. Some CRMs are free to use until your database reaches a certain size, at which time a subscription fee is required.

Once you have chosen a type of database to use, you need to choose how you will set it up. Databases have "records", which are electronic forms on which information on one particular person, company, or item is stored within the database. Within each record are "fields" in which individual pieces of data, such as name or telephone number, can be stored. Most databases allow you to choose which types of fields to use and offer the option of creating custom fields. It is suggested that your database include the following fields at a minimum:

- Company or Organization Name.
- Company Address.
- Company Main Telephone Number.
- Contact Name.
- Contact Title (Security Director, Facility Manager, VP Finance, etc.)
- Contact Direct Telephone Number.
- Contact Email.
- Industry (Healthcare, manufacturing, financial services, etc.)
- Contact Type (Prospect, past client, influencer, etc.)
- Status (Ready to call, appointment set, call back later, etc.)
- Notes (General information, record of conversations, etc.)

Many additional fields can be added if you want. These may include company size, number of company employees, company's annual sales, locations of field offices, etc. This additional information can allow you to create targeted marketing campaigns that focus only on prospects of a certain type and size.

Filling Your Database with Prospects

Once you have created your marketing database, you need to go about filling it with data.

Start out by entering prospects that you already know about and already have full information on. These are people that you personally know and have already established relationships with through past jobs, professional associations, and community activities. Information on these people can be gleaned from your personal contact files and that stack of business cards that you have gathering dust somewhere.

After you have the easy ones out of the way, you need to begin to gather the names of other prospects that you don't already know but would like to establish relationships with and sell your services to. For the beginning consultant, these people will make up the large majority of their marketing database.

How do you find these people? To answer this question, you need to step back and ask yourself a few questions first:

- What is my chosen area of practice? (Security management consultant specializing in hospitals, technical security consultant specializing in government facilities, etc.)
- What types of companies or organizations are most likely to need my services? (Corporations, law firms, non-profit organizations, government agencies, hospitals, schools, etc.)
- What size companies or organizations are most likely to hire me? (Small businesses, multinational corporations, hospitals with greater than 500 beds, non-profits with revenue in excess of ten million, cities with populations in excess of one million, etc.)
- What geographical areas can I most effectively serve? (Los Angeles metropolitan area, State of California, Western United States, etc.) When defining the geographical area in which you wish to market to, consider your ability to provide services to the client in a cost-effective manner, as well as your ability to make in-person sales calls to prospective clients.
- Who are the likely decision makers at the companies or organizations that I am targeting? (Security Directors, Facility Managers, Human Resources Directors, etc.)

The answers to these questions will obviously vary greatly depending on your area of practice and individual circumstances. Here are a couple of examples:

Example #1

Area of Practice and Service Offerings

Security management consultant that serves hospitals and healthcare institutions. I provide security assessments, policies and procedures development, and security awareness training.

Type of Client I Am Targeting

- Hospitals
- Outpatient Clinics

Size of Client I Am Targeting

- Large-Sized Hospitals (>500 beds)
- Medium-Sized Hospitals (250 to 500 beds)
- Medical Clinics with 3 or more locations.

Geographical Region

Connecticut, Maine, Massachusetts, New Hampshire, Rhode Island and Vermont.

Likely Decision Makers

- Security or Public Safety Director
- Facilities Director
- VP Support Services

Example #2

Area of Practice and Service Offerings

Technical security consultant that serves courthouses, law enforcement agencies, and state and local government agencies. I design and specify electronic security systems and oversee the installation of these systems.

Type of Client I Am Targeting

- City governments.
- County governments.
- Architectural and engineering (A/E) firms that specialize in government facilities and courthouses.

Size of Client I Am Targeting

- Cities with a population greater than 500,000.
- Counties with a population greater than 1,000,000.
- A/E Firms with billing greater than $1,000,000 annually.

Geographical Region

California and Nevada

Likely Decision Makers

Facility Directors.

Security Managers.

Principals at A/E Firms.

Marketing Specialists at A/E Firms.

By answering the questions above, you have established the general criteria for the type of prospect that you are seeking. You now need to find the specific prospects that meet this criteria. It is suggested this be done in two steps:

Step #1 – Find Companies and Organizations

The first step is to find the companies and organizations that meet your criteria. Fortunately, this has never been easier due to the multitude of online resources on the internet. There are numerous industry directories of various types of companies and organizations, as well as regional directories that list companies and organizations by geographical region. Often, newspapers and magazines will create lists such as "Top 25 Hospitals in Cleveland" or "Major Employers in Orange County" that can be found by doing a simple online search.

After your searches have identified companies and organizations that meet your criteria, begin creating database records for each one. Many directory listings will provide the information necessary to complete the Company Name, Company Address, and Main Company Telephone Number fields in your database. If not, go to the website of the specific company or organization to obtain this information.

This step will produce accurate information for probably about 90% of the companies and organizations that fit your criteria. When researching companies that have multiple locations, searches will most likely produce information on their main location or headquarters. Finding information on their local or regional locations may require a little more effort.

Step #2 – Find the Right Contact People

The second step is to identify the specific people within each company that meet your criteria. This can be very easy or very difficult depending on the specific types of industries you are targeting and the specific job titles that you wish to obtain information on.

In general, obtaining information on top level management is easy – this is often listed on the company website or available through directories of various types. Finding information on lower-level management and other employees can be more challenging.

When searching for contact people, using the following techniques may produce results:

1. A simple internet search using the right terms can often yield remarkable results. For example, doing a search with company name and department ("XYZ Company" + "Facilities") can produce results from news articles, internal company newsletters, charitable organization events, license and permit applications, and many other sources. Get creative and have fun with it and it's surprising what you may find.
2. Look through the on-line directories of the various types of associations that your contact may belong to; for example,

many security directors belong to ASIS, many facility managers belong to IFMA or BOMA, etc. There is almost always an association that represents any job title that you are targeting. Get to know the appropriate associations for the types of clients you are targeting. (You may need to become a member of some of these associations in order to gain access to their directories.)

3. Search listings on business networking sites such as LinkedIn.
4. If you have a relationship with someone at another organization with a similar job title, call them and ask if they know the name of their counterpart at the company you are targeting.
5. If nothing else works, try calling the main telephone number of the company and just asking. Many companies have mechanisms in place to thwart unsolicited calls, but you can often obtain the information you are seeking if you use a little finesse.

As you identify contact names for each of the companies that you are targeting, enter them into your database. In many cases, you will be lucky enough to get the contact's telephone number and email address from the same source from which you obtained the name. If so, enter these in your database.

If you have a contact name, but not a phone number or email address, you will need to make additional efforts to find this information using the techniques described above.

In some cases, email addresses can be found by doing an internet search using the term "Fred Fictitious" + @xyxcompany.com", where Fred Fictitious is the name of the contact and XYZ Company is the name of the company preceded by the @ sign. In other cases, email addresses can be deduced by looking at the format used in other known email addresses for the company. For example, by looking at the email "john.smith@xyzcompany.com", you can probably assume that

Fred Fictitious' s email is "fred.fictitious@xyzcompany.com". This technique is always worth a try if you run into a dead-end.

As you create your database, you will always come across companies for which you cannot find the name of a suitable contact. You will also have the names of contacts for whom you cannot find a telephone number or email address for. Keep the records for these companies in your database but indicate in the status field that the record is incomplete. As time goes on, you will inevitably come across sources of information that allow you to fill in the missing pieces.

As you can see, filling your database with prospects can be a time-consuming process. It can take a new consultant several months to build an effective marketing database and fill it with prospects. Effective databases are built gradually name-by-name and will continue to grow throughout the life of your consulting practice. I add new names and missing information to my database on almost a daily basis.

Filling Your Database with Influencers

Influencers are people who may not buy your services themselves but can refer you to prospects who can. Who your influencers are will vary depending on your specific practice areas. When choosing influencers to include in your database, ask yourself the following questions:

- "Who are clients likely to first contact when they have a problem involving my area of expertise?"
- "Who is likely to first hear about opportunities where services of my type are needed?"
- "Who might the client mistakenly call when they need services of my type?"
- "Who offers services of my type but may turn-away projects when they are too busy or feel that the project is too small?"
- "Who provides services in allied fields that are closely related to my own?"

Here is an example of some of the influencers in my marketing database:

- Accountants and auditors.
- Audio/video consultants.
- Electrical engineers.
- Fire protection consultants.
- Guard companies.
- Hardware consultants.
- Cybersecurity consultants.
- Insurance brokers.
- Locksmiths.
- Manufacturer's representatives.
- Police crime prevention officers.
- Private investigators.
- Project management firms.
- Security product distributors.
- Security systems integrators.

Many people starting their consulting practice will probably find that they already have contact information on many influencers from their previous jobs. To locate new influencers, use the same types of techniques that were used to find prospects that were described above.

Once you are established, you will find that many influencers will seek you out, hoping that you can also help them. It is acceptable for you to make referrals to your influencers, provided that there is no potential for a conflict of interest.

When receiving a referral from someone who sells security products or services, I make it clear that I always look out for the best interests of the client, regardless of who referred me to the business.

This has resulted in situations where I advised a client to hire someone other than the company that recommended me – obviously making the person who referred me very unhappy. To maintain my independence, I never agree to "quid pro quo" arrangements where I accept referrals provided that I agree to send business to the referring company in return.

Influencers should be entered in your marketing database just like prospects but should be separately flagged in the Contact Type field.

Filling Your Database with Past Clients

Past clients are people that you have provided security consulting services to in the past. Past clients can be both prospects for additional services, and influencers who can refer you to other prospects.

When you are starting out, you probably won't have any past clients to enter in your database. As you begin to sell projects, some people who were in your database as prospects now become past clients and their flag in the Contact Type field should be changed accordingly. New clients that were not already in your database should also be added as their project is completed.

Paid Sources of Information

There are numerous companies that will sell you mailing lists and leads to use in your marketing campaigns. Some consultants may choose to fill their marketing database quickly using information from these sources. There are also companies that provide access to contact information directories on a paid basis.

I have used these sources of information in the past with mixed results. In some cases, the information received was good, but in other cases, no information was available on the companies I was targeting, or the information provided was hopelessly outdated.

I personally no longer use services of this type, but you may find them effective for the types of contacts that you are searching for. You can usually subscribe to these services on a trial basis for free or for a small charge.

Growing Your Database

You should continue to grow your marketing database on a continual basis. There are sources of leads and information everywhere. For example, when reading the business newspapers in my area, I frequently come across press releases announcing the start of new businesses or giving the names of people who have been promoted to new jobs at existing businesses. When appropriate, I enter the names of these companies and people in my database. I also add people that I have met at events that I feel would be good prospects or influencers. I also scan LinkedIn, online forums, and blogs to identify new leads to add to my database.

Working Your Database

Once you have established your marketing database, you need to begin mining it. It is recommended that some type of communication be made with every prospective client, past client, and influencer at least twice per year. These communications can occur by direct mail, by email, by telephone, or by in-person visits.

When you are just starting your consulting practice, working your database should be your primary job – you should get up each morning and begin communicating with the people in your database, as well as locating new people to add to your database. This should go on day after day, week after week until your practice starts to gain traction.

After you begin to get consulting projects, you can reduce the amount of time that you spend mining your database, but you should never stop. Even the very busiest of consultants should try to spend at least several hours per week making contacts using their marketing database.

Don't expect to see immediate results. It can sometimes take months or even years until the seeds that you plant by working your database begin to bear fruit. But bear fruit they surely will if you are persistent enough.

When I started my practice, I immediately initiated a direct mail campaign to architects, engineers, and security managers in my market area. In less than two weeks, I received a small project from an electrical engineer who contacted me after receiving my direct mail letter. I later went on to perform many additional projects for this same engineer. Ultimately, I received over $50,000 in consulting fees as a result of this one direct mail letter.

What is even more interesting is that, five years later, I received a call from an architect who had received a direct mail letter from my very first campaign. He started the conversation saying, "*Are you still doing that security consulting*?" and proceeded to describe a project in Alaska that he needed help with. This architect filed my brochure away in case he had a need for security consulting in the future, and sure enough, five years later, he did. As a result of a letter I sent five years earlier, I was awarded a very interesting and profitable project.

Mining your database will yield results if you are persistent enough to stick with it. The more contacts that you make using your database, the better your results will be.

Just out of curiosity, I recently went back to an archival copy of my first database and compared it to my current list of past and present clients. A surprising number of clients that eventually hired me were in my original database, confirming that my method of targeting potential clients was largely effective. While some of these clients found me in another way, a good percentage hired me specifically because of my marketing campaigns.

Direct Mail Campaigns

Direct mail campaigns are a time-tested way to reach potential clients. Direct mail campaigns involve sending letters to people in your marketing database using US Mail. Some consultants may claim that in this era of electronic communications, mailing letters is outdated and ineffective, but I feel just the opposite. Because fewer and fewer businesses are mailing letters, I feel that the impact of receiving a letter is greater than it has ever been.

However, in order to have this impact, the letter must look like a piece of personal correspondence, not just another piece of junk mail. To achieve this, the following is suggested:

1. Letters should be written on your letterhead and printed on high-quality paper.
2. Letters should be sent in a high-quality business envelope.
3. Letter and envelope should be individually addressed using the name and job title of the contact at the company you are targeting.

4. An individual First-Class postage stamp should be affixed to the envelope. Using a postage meter, or worse yet, a flat-rate mail permit, can make your letter look like junk mail.
5. The letter should be very short, three or four paragraphs maximum. Within the letter, you should introduce yourself, briefly describe the services that you offer, and indicate what action you would like the recipient to take.
6. Use simple, conversational language in your letter, like you were writing to a friend.
7. The letter should be personally signed by you in ink.
8. The letter should include your business card.

A simple trifold type of brochure can also be included in the letter, but just a letter and business card can be remarkably effective. The more material that you provide in the envelope, the less that it looks like a personal letter.

The cost of mailing a direct mail letter currently runs between one and two dollars per letter. While somewhat expensive, I feel that using direct mail is one of the better ways for an independent security consultant to generate business. Even if only one out of a hundred people respond to your letters, the money spent is a relatively small price to pay to get a new consulting client.

Some consultants do mass mailings using preprinted postcards as a way to save money. I have not personally used postcards but suspect that the rate of return when using them is only a fraction of that achieved when using a direct mail letter. Doing something that costs less, but has a lower rate of return, can actually cost more money in the long run.

The success of any direct mail campaign is directly linked to the quality of the names in your marketing database. If you have done a good job of qualifying your prospects when developing your database, your rate of return will be much higher than if you use just any list of names.

(Example of direct mail letter to company owner from security management consultant.)

June 5, 2024

Mr. John Doe
Owner
Acme Corporation
123 Main Street
Detroit, MI 48201

Dear John,

Have you been experiencing thefts or other losses at your company? Are you concerned about the safety and security of your employees?

If so, I think I can be of help to you.

I am an independent security consultant that has been serving clients in Detroit for more than 25 years. I don't sell security systems or guard services - but provide objective, professional advice on how you can better protect your people, information, and other assets. I can help you to reduce losses, decrease security operating costs and keep you from spending money on security equipment that really isn't needed.

Please contact me to arrange a free, no-obligation meeting to discuss ways in which I can help you to improve your security.

Sincerely,

Joe Smith
XYZ Consultants

(Example of direct mail letter to property manager from security management consultant.)

June 5, 2024

Ms. Sally Strong
Senior Property Manager
Acme Management
123 Main Street
Detroit, MI 48201

Dear Sally,

As a property manager, your clients often come to you when they are experiencing thefts, vandalism, and other types of crimes.

Do you ever wish you had someone to turn to when you had a security question? Someone who could give you expert security advice without trying to sell you something? If so, perhaps I can be of help.

I am an independent security consultant that has been serving clients in Detroit for more than 25 years. I don't sell security systems or guard services - but provide objective, professional advice on how you can better protect the people, information, and other assets at the properties you manage. I can help you to reduce losses, decrease security operating costs, and keep you from spending money on security systems that aren't really needed.

Please contact me to arrange a free, no-obligation meeting to discuss ways in which I can help you to improve the security at the properties that you are responsible for.

Sincerely,

Joe Smith
XYZ Consultants

(Example of direct mail letter to architect from technical security consultant.)

June 5, 2024

Mr. Tom Creative
Principal in Charge
Creative Architects
123 Main Street
Detroit, MI 48201

Dear Tom,

I am an independent security consultant in the Detroit area that specializes in the design and planning of electronic security systems such as access control systems, video surveillance systems, alarm monitoring systems, and security communications systems.

I am completely independent and do not sell or install security equipment. I regularly work with architects such as yourself to incorporate the design of security systems into new construction and renovation projects.

I want to be the security consultant on your next project. Please contact me to arrange a free, no-obligation meeting to discuss ways in which having a qualified security consultant on your team can help you to win more projects and to better serve your clients.

Sincerely,

Joe Smith
XYZ Consultants

Email Campaigns

Sending email messages costs almost nothing, and as a result, is a popular marketing technique used by nearly every type of business. Unfortunately, the ease with which unsolicited email messages can be sent has led to significant abuse, giving email marketing a bad name, and causing laws to be passed regulating the use of email in marketing. Unsolicited email is often known as "spam".

When using email in marketing campaigns, there are three common scenarios:

> <u>Scenario #1</u>
>
> You have obtained the email address of a prospect from a prior business relationship or from an inquiry from the prospect.
>
> <u>Scenario #2</u>
>
> The prospect has "opted-in" to receive email from you by subscribing to your blog or website or by filling out and submitting a written request.
>
> <u>Scenario #3</u>
>
> You have obtained the email address of a prospect, but you have no present or prior business relationship with the prospect, and you want to send them an unsolicited email.

Scenarios #1 and #2 rarely create problems because the person receiving the email knows who you are and usually not surprised to receive correspondence from you. These scenarios apply when you are sending emails to influencers and past clients in your database, making email a good way to stay in touch with this type of contact.

Scenario #3, where you are sending unsolicited emails to a person that you don't already know, is the one that is the most regulated by law and has the most potential to cause you trouble. However, this scenario is the one that will most likely apply when you want to reach the new prospects that are contained in your marketing database.

I feel that sending unsolicited emails to prospects can be an effective marketing strategy if it is done with extreme care. When planning an email campaign that involves the sending of unsolicited emails, the following should be considered:

- Fully understand and comply with the laws concerning the use of email in marketing as they apply in your country. In the United States, a law known as the "CAN-SPAM Act" regulates the use of email in commerce.
- Understand any rules that your internet service provider (ISP) has concerning the sending of unsolicited emails. Sometimes, these rules may be even stricter than those imposed by law. A complaint to your ISP from a person receiving an unsolicited email can result in the cancellation of your internet account.
- Always use your real name, address and telephone number in your messages.
- Make it easy for a recipient to "opt-out" if they no longer wish to receive your messages. Promptly honor these requests.
- Limit the number of unsolicited emails that you send to any prospect to only one or two per year.

The message contained within your unsolicited email should be similar to the message used in your direct mail letters. This message should be specifically tailored to the type of prospect that you are trying to reach.

Email messages offer the added advantage of allowing you to insert "links" to your website and articles that may be of interest to your prospect. For example, when sending emails to property managers, you could include a link to a short article you have written called "*Ten Security Tips for Property Managers*". Including links that are of benefit to the recipient is one way to increase the effectiveness of your email campaign. But be careful – adding more than a couple of links in a short message can get your message flagged as "spam" by spam filters.

The words to use in the subject line of your email messages is a hotly debated topic among marketing professionals. I personally prefer to use subject lines that are short and to the point. An example of email subject lines that I have used in the past include "*Need Help with Security?*", "*Are You Doing Enough to Keep Your Employees Safe?*", "*I Want to Be Your Security Guy*", and "*Making Your Next Security Project Go Smoothly*".

Some consultants send unsolicited emails using a full page of text and graphics. These are often called "HTML emails" and look just like a webpage when viewed on most devices. I personally prefer to send simple, plain-text emails that look just like a message from a business associate or friend. I feel that these have a better chance of being read and acted upon.

There are commercial email services such as Constant Contact and Mail Chimp that allow your marketing email process to be fully automated. These services require that all recipient's "opt-in" in order to receive messages, making them ideal for sending mailings to influencers and past clients. These services are also great for sending out electronic newsletters. Because of their prohibitions on sending messages to people who have not opted-in, these services are not suitable for sending unsolicited emails.

Telephone Campaigns

One way to strike terror in the heart of most new security consultants is to ask them to pick up the phone and call a prospective client that they do not know. This is often known as "cold calling", and along with public speaking, is one of the things that people fear most. Even seasoned security professionals who have previous law enforcement experience seem like they would rather engage in a gun battle with a violent suspect than pick up the phone and call an unknown person.

Making unsolicited telephone calls is also perceived negatively by many new consultants, who think of themselves as security experts rather than salesmen or peddlers. Many also fear the rejection that they will encounter when making unsolicited calls.

Despite the fear and loathing around making cold calls, this technique is the single most effective one that you can use to get new business. While the technique works particularly well when combined with other efforts such as direct mail campaigns, just using the telephone alone can produce incredible results.

The first step in making effective calls is to get yourself in the right mindset. First, you must strongly believe in the consulting services that you are selling. Reflect on what you do and the value that it provides to the client. The services offered by most security consultants reduce losses, prevent injuries and even help to save lives. Your services should be something that you are proud of and eager to share with your potential clients.

Second, reflect on the reasons that you became an independent security consultant in the first place. Whether it is to earn a good living, gain satisfaction by doing what you are good at, or to establish a reputation in the industry, you have goals. Achieving these goals requires getting projects, and getting projects requires making telephone calls. Remember, you are making these calls for you and your family, not anyone else.

Third, understand that calling is a numbers game. While the majority of the people that you call may reject you or put you off, some percentage of the people that you reach will have an actual need for your services and will appreciate your call. You only need to reach a small number of these people each year in order to be successful. The more people that you call, the better your chances of reaching the right people will be.

Fourth, understand that rejection is just part of the game. Don't take it personally. While most people that you call will be pleasant, some may be rude or downright abusive. Remember that this type of behavior is the other person's problem, not yours. Consider difficult people to be just like turbulence on a plane flight – a few bumps during an otherwise pleasant trip, and nothing that will prevent you from reaching your destination.

Fifth, understand that making telephone calls will get easier with time. You will eventually develop a rhythm and perfect your techniques. This can take a couple of hundred calls to achieve, but it will eventually happen, and things will be much easier from then on. Many consultants who once dreaded making cold calls now find that it is one of the most enjoyable things that they do.

Before making a telephone call, it is recommended that you write a short "script" that outlines what you want to say. Novice callers don't see the need to do this and try to ad lib or handle the call on the fly, while experienced callers always work from some type of script.

Before preparing your script, identify the purpose of your call. Do you just want to make the prospect aware of your services so they can call when there is a need, or do you want to sell a specific service right now? Are you trying to sell directly to this prospect, or simply trying to get a referral to another buyer?

Once you have identified the purpose of your call, you can begin to write your script. Here is an example of a script that could be used when a security management consultant was calling a facility manager at a company without a security department:

Consultant

"Hello, John, this is Joe Smith from XYZ Consultants. "Is this a bad time to call?"

Prospect

"No, I can talk for a few minutes.

Consultant

"Good. John, you may not have heard of me, but I am an independent security consultant that has been operating in the Detroit area for the last 25 years. I don't sell any type of security product or guard service, allowing me to be completely independent. I understand that you are responsible for facilities at your company. Let me ask you, are you responsible for managing the security function at your company as well?"

Prospect

"Yeah, I handle security, safety, and nearly everything else related to the upkeep of the facility.

Consultant

"Great. It sounds like you have your hands full in handling security along with all of your other responsibilities". Tell me, what are the biggest security challenges that you are presently facing?" (Listen carefully, asking questions if needed to better understand the prospect's concerns.)

Prospect

"We have had very few security problems over the years, but recently we have had a large number of break-ins of cars in the employee parking garage. I'm also concerned about all of the events going on in the news lately and wondering what we would do if someone came in with a gun."

Consultant

"I certainly understand your concerns. Thefts in the parking garage can make employees nervous about their safety. And recent events in the news can definitely make you want to review your security measures to see if you are taking reasonable steps to protect your employees. If it's any consolation, many of my other clients have experienced issues similar to your own, and I have been able to help them to identify some cost-effective ways to address them. Have you ever worked with an independent security consultant before?"

Prospect

"No. We had a vendor come out last month to give us a quote on installing cameras in the parking garage, but the company president didn't want to spend any money. Our guard company also suggested that we post an additional guard in the garage, but I'm not sure how much good this would do".

Consultant

"Cameras and guards can be useful tools but are not a security solution in themselves. I would suggest that you take a "big picture" look at security before you spend any money on cameras or more security guards.

We have a process known as a "security assessment" that takes a comprehensive look at all of your security needs. This process identifies your security risks and threats, examines your existing systems and procedures, and identifies cost effective ways in which security at your facility can be improved.

This security assessment can be used as a long-range plan to help you to prioritize your security investments. Do you think that your facility would benefit from having an assessment of this type done?"

Prospect

"Yeah, I think that doing something like that would be a good idea. What does it cost?

Consultant

"John, if you will permit me, I would like to come by for a quick visit to further explain the security assessment process and learn a little more about your business. After this visit, I will be able to provide you with a written proposal that provides a detailed scope of work along with a firm estimate of costs. There is no obligation on your part, and you can decide whether or not to proceed after you review the proposal. I am available to meet with you on either Tuesday afternoon or Thursday morning next week. Which of these would work best for you?"

Prospect

"Tuesday afternoon would work best for me".

Consultant

"Great, let's plan on meeting at 2:00 on Tuesday of next week".

Prospect

"Come to the main lobby and ask the receptionist to page me".

Consultant

"Wonderful. I look forward to meeting you on Tuesday".

Please note that within the script above, the prospect raised no objections. In real-world calls, this is not always the case, therefore, your script should anticipate objections and come up with appropriate responses. Here are some examples of objections and responses:

Prospect Objection

"Yes, this is a really bad time to call".

Consultant Response

"I'm sorry. When would be a good time to call you back?" (Make a note in your calendar of when to call back.)

Prospect Objection

"No, I don't handle security. It's part of the Safety Manager's responsibilities".

Consultant Response

"Thank you for that information. Can you tell me the name and number of the Safety Manager?" (Update your database with this information and call the Safety Manager.)

Prospect Objection

"We are actually owned by the Acme Conglomerate and all of our security needs are handled by the Acme Corporate Security Department".

Consultant Response

"It sounds like your security needs are being well-taken care of by your security department. Do you happen to know the name of your contact at Corporate Security?" (Update your database with this information and contact Corporate Security to see if they ever use the services of local independent security consultants.)

Prospect Objection

"Our security guard company, Zebra Security, also acts as our security consultant".

Consultant Response

"Zebra is an excellent company and very knowledgeable about security guards, but most guard companies are not well-versed in all aspects of security management. Also, there is always the potential for a conflict of interest when a consultant who recommends a security product or service just happens to be the one that sells it. John, if you will permit me, I would like to come by for a quick visit to further explain the benefits of using an independent security consultant. Would Tuesday of next week be convenient?"

Prospect Objection

"We use Abe Vigoda, an independent security consultant out of Atlanta, to handle our security consulting needs".

Consultant Response

"Abe is a highly qualified consultant and has an excellent reputation. I'm glad that you found someone of his caliber to work with. Thanks for taking the time to talk with me". (My personal policy is to not go after the clients of other independent security consultants. You may choose to take a different approach.)

Prospect Objection

"We haven't had any security problems whatsoever". We don't see any need for your services at this time."

Consultant Response

"I'm glad to hear that you haven't had any problems. I would appreciate it if you would keep me in mind if you do have a need in the future. By the way, I frequently publish free articles that offer security tips for companies such as yours. With your permission, I would like to add you to my mailing list and send these articles to you from time to time. May I have your email address?" (Add to your database and flag record to indicate that prospect has "opted-in" to receive emails from you.)

It can take time and effort to develop an effective script for each type of prospect that you call, but once developed, scripts can be used over and over and fine-tuned to address new objections that prospects may raise. Over time, using your scripts will become second nature.

A few final tips when making marketing telephone calls:

- When first introducing yourself to a prospect, try to find a common connection between you and the prospect. These common connections can include:
    - The name of the person that suggested that you call the prospect (*"Bob at the ABC Company suggested that I call you."*)
    - The name of an association that both you and the prospect belong to (*"I noticed that you and I are both members of the Moss Bay Chapter of ASIS"*).
    - The name of a client that is one of your prospect's peers (*"I just completed a project for Mercy Hospital, which as you know, is the only other Level 1 Trauma Center in the state and very similar to your own hospital"*)
    - The name of a client that is in close vicinity to the prospect's facility *("I just completed a security assessment for Ace Laboratories, which is located directly across the street from your plant."*)
- Try to keep a smile on your face when you are calling. Imagine that you are talking with a family member or close friend that you really like. While this may sound silly to some, how you feel when making a call can have a big impact on how your message is received on the other end.
- Try to spend as much time listening as you spend talking. Really listen when the prospect talks – don't be spending this time thinking about what you will say next.
- Never interrupt a prospect. Always acknowledge what the prospect has said before making a reply.

- Don't overwhelm the prospect with too much information. There is no need to provide information on all of your qualifications, experience, project history, and service offerings during a single call. Have a specific objective for each call, and when this objective is met, conclude the call.
- If you reach voice mail when calling, leave a message. Don't try to read your whole script, but instead say who you are, describe what you do, and leave a callback number. Even if the prospect never calls you back, you have made an impression.
- When a particular prospect seems difficult to reach, try calling an hour before or after the company's stated business hours. Busy people are often in their office early or late and can be especially receptive to calls at this time.
- Try not to get cornered into quoting prices or agreeing to a specific scope of work during your first marketing call with a prospect. While it is OK to quote a general range of fees (*"A security assessment of this type typically costs between $7,000 and $15,000"*), try not to get pinned down on costs until you have had a chance to review the client's requirements and prepare a proposal.

In-Person Sales Calls

In-person sales calls are a golden opportunity to present your qualifications and to sell your services. The sales call is an important steppingstone in the path that leads to obtaining a consulting contract with a client. The purpose of all of your other marketing efforts should be to create opportunities to schedule in-person sales calls.

New security consultants are encouraged to go on as many in-person sales calls as possible. There is no better way to learn about the actual security needs of prospects and just how well your proposed service offerings are being received by the market. Sales calls also provide you with direct exposure to buyers and give you the opportunity to further develop your sales and presentation skills. As your consulting practice becomes more successful, you may choose to be more selective about the type of sales calls that you go on, but at the start, I would suggest that you go on every call that you can.

Sales calls are initiated in one of two ways. The first way is when the prospect calls you. These calls happen when someone refers the prospect to you, or when the prospect calls you in response to one of your marketing campaigns or after visiting your website. These sales calls are the preferred type as you are there at the prospect's request, giving you somewhat of an advantage.

The second way that sales calls are initiated is when you ask for an appointment during one of your marketing telephone calls. Getting the prospect to agree to an in-person visit is a big step in the sales process, but you usually need to work a little harder during this type of call because it was you who initiated the visit.

The goal of sales calls is to sell the prospect on both you and your services. In some cases, the prospect has already decided to use the services of a consultant and is now trying to determine if you are the right consultant to hire. In these cases, your only job is to convince the prospect that you are a better choice than all of the other consultants that the prospect is considering.

In other cases, the prospective client may not yet be convinced that they need to hire a consultant at all. In these cases, you must first convince the prospect of the advantages of using an independent security consultant over the other alternative sources of advice that may be available. After having sold the concept of using a consultant, you then need to sell yourself.

Here are a few suggestions on making in-person sales calls:

- Always do your homework on the prospect prior to going on the sales call. Learn about the organization, its products and services, and where its facilities are located. Also search for any recent news articles about the organization. With all of the sources of information available on the internet today, there is absolutely no excuse for not being informed.

- Dress in a professional and businesslike manner. You should never be dressed more casually than the people you are selling to, but the opposite is usually OK – clients expect professionals to be professionally dressed. When in doubt, dress more formally rather than more casually during your first visit. If you see that everyone at the prospect's facility is dressed casually, you can dress down at subsequent meetings.

- Know where you are going in advance. Allow plenty of time to get there, even in bad traffic. Being late is never acceptable.
- Arrive 15-30 minutes early for your appointment. Take a few minutes to relax, cool down, and get prepared. Make a final check of your appearance in a mirror before you walk into your interview.
- Act the part of a serious professional advisor, like a doctor or lawyer. While you should be friendly, don't be overly familiar with the prospect and never try to be a comedian.
- Always start by thanking the prospect for giving you the opportunity to meet. Ask how much time is available so that you can pace your presentation to fit the allotted time. Never exceed the stated time limit unless the prospect requests it.
- Be a good listener. The meeting should be a conversation, not a monologue. Even when making a presentation, solicit feedback from the prospect along the way and encourage participation.
- End the meeting by confirming what the next step in the process will be. If you intend to follow up with a proposal, tell this to the prospect and provide a specific deadline as to when you will have the proposal to the prospect. *("John, I will have the proposal to you no later than noon on Friday".)*
- Once you get back to your office, send an email to the prospect again thanking them for their time and confirming any follow-up actions required.
- Always promptly honor any commitments that you made during the meeting. Making small commitments and honoring them is one way to establish trust with a prospective client. Being late in delivering on promises and making excuses about it has the opposite effect.

Out of Town Prospects

When a prospect is located in the same city as you are, or a reasonable driving distance away, in-person sales calls are practical. But what do you do when a prospect is located in another city, perhaps hundreds or even thousands of miles away?

Some consultants who serve multiple cities set aside days in each city specifically to make in-person sales calls. This is most cost effective when done at the beginning or end of a paid consulting project, but there may be times when it makes sense to make a special trip just for marketing purposes.

When coming across a potential opportunity located a long way from home, consultants have a business decision to make: are the potential rewards in making a trip to visit the prospective client worth the costs involved? Because of the substantial costs of business travel, the new consultant can't afford to get the answer to this question wrong too many times.

When evaluating a potential opportunity that involves an investment in out-of-town travel, ask yourself the following:

- Was I referred to this prospect by a past client or influencer, or did I come across the opportunity in another way?
- Am I likely the only consultant being considered for the project, or is the prospect openly soliciting proposals from other consultants?
- Am I likely competing with other consultants who are located closer and may be able to provide services more cost effectively?
- What is the potential value of the project in relation to the travel costs involved?
- Is this a one-time project, or is there likely an opportunity for lots of future work?

For example, if the consultant was referred to the prospect by a satisfied past client, the consultant was the only one being considered, the project involved a large consulting fee, and there was potential for lots of future work , it would be worth the investment to make an out-of-town sales call.

On the other hand, if the project was of relatively small size, there was little potential for future work, and the consultant was competing with many other consultants located closer to the project, it would very likely not be worth the investment.

Many new consultants are overly optimistic about their chances of success in winning a project, spend lots of money pursuing it, and then are deeply disappointed (and have a lot less money) when the opportunity falls through. Use your head and not your heart when evaluating potential opportunities.

Sales Calls Using Video Conferencing

When it is not cost-effective to make an in-person sales call to a prospect, selling using video conferencing is the next best thing. There are numerous video platforms such as Google Meet, Microsoft Teams, Webex, and Zoom that allow you to make video conference calls where you can not only communicate with your prospect but make high-quality presentations using videos and slide shows. Many of these platforms offer a limited version of their service for free, and a full featured version at a moderate cost.

The use of video conferencing platforms became commonplace during the pandemic of 2020 and are now a widely accepted means of business communications.

When conducting a video conference, follow the same rules that apply to an in-person sales call. Dress appropriately and act professionally. Be sure that the room in which you are conducting the call is not cluttered and that there are no distractions in the background.

If you plan to regularly make video conference calls, it is recommended that you purchase a high-quality external webcam that includes a stereo microphone. These provide much better results than the camera and microphone that is built into most computers.

As useful as video conferencing is, I still consider it to be less effective than an in-person sales call. There is nothing like making actual person-to-person contact with a prospect. For these reasons, I would always choose an in-person visit over a video conference when it is cost effective.

Networking with Influencers

Influencers are people who may not buy your services themselves but can refer you to prospects who can. Influencers are an important source of leads for most security consultants. Over time, you can establish relationships with hundreds of influencers, each of which has access to a different segment of prospects, helping you to greatly leverage your marketing efforts.

I personally have benefited greatly from influencers, and some of my biggest and most profitable projects over the years have come from this source.

You should make deliberate efforts to constantly grow your network of influencers, and to stay in touch with influencers that you already have relationships with. By regularly communicating with influencers, you keep you and your service offerings fresh in their minds, making it more likely that they will recommend you when they encounter someone who has a need.

It is recommended that you contact each influencer in your database at least twice per year. A telephone call works best, but a quick email can also be effective. It is also recommended that you meet in person with your important influencers whenever possible. I try to meet with influencers for coffee or lunch periodically throughout the year, particularly when I am working in an area near where they are located.

Always take the time to thank an influencer when they refer a potential client to you – even if the referral doesn't result in a sale. I always do this with a telephone call rather than an email or text message, expressing sincere thanks for the referral and telling them to "keep them coming".

Networking with Past Clients

Past clients are people that you have provided security consulting services to in the past. Past clients can be both prospects for additional services, and influencers who can refer you to other prospects. Past clients can also be used as references to help you to obtain projects from new clients.

Because of all that they can potentially do for you, past clients should be considered some of the most cherished people in your marketing database. Yet, it is amazing how many consultants seem to completely ignore their past clients after they complete the initial project that the client hired them to do.

You should not make this mistake. Develop an active program to regularly reach out to your past clients. The following is suggested:

- Call or visit past clients at least twice per year. If possible, make an in-person visit to each past client at least once per year.
- During each call or visit, ask the client about any new security issues or problems that the client may be experiencing.
- Remind past clients about additional services that you can provide. For example, if you recently completed a security assessment for a client, remind them that you can also help them with writing security policies and procedures or developing an RFP for a new security system.
- Ask the client if they know of any people at other companies who might benefit from your services. For example, most facilities managers know some or all of their counterparts at other companies and are usually glad to provide an introduction if asked. But you must ask – they are unlikely to do this on their own.
- Be willing to provide a limited number of services to past clients at no charge. For example, when one of my past clients calls me with a question that takes me 30 minutes to research, I don't usually send them a bill for this time.

- When making an in-person visit to a client contact, try to get to meet as many people in your contact's department as possible, particularly anyone who may be in line to take your contact's job when they leave. It is not uncommon for a contact person to retire or move on to another job, sometimes leaving a consultant with no connection to a client that they have previously done business with.
- If a past client seems particularly satisfied with your services, ask them to provide you with a written letter of recommendation. Most clients are happy to do this if asked. Over time, you will accumulate an impressive number of letters that can be used in marketing materials and proposals.

Reaching Out to Competitors

Competitors are other security consultants and security consulting firms that provide some or all of the same services that you do. Although completely counter-intuitive, your competitors can actually be a good source of work.

Many times, a competitor will come across a project that is too small or too large for them to handle, and they need someone to refer the client to. In other cases, the competitor may be simply too busy to take on new work or have a conflict of interest that prevents them from working for a specific client.

When starting your consulting practice, reach out to any known competitors in your market area. Introduce yourself and the services that you provide. Ask that the competitor consider referring clients to you when they come across a project that they don't want to handle and offer to do the same thing for them. I think that you will be pleasantly surprised at just how receptive your competitors are to this type of arrangement. You may even find yourself being offered work as a subcontractor to a larger consulting firm.

Association Meetings

Many independent security consultants join professional associations related to their area of practice. For example, most security consultants choose to join ASIS, the leading association for security professionals. Consultants specializing in hospitals and healthcare might join the International Association for Healthcare Security and Safety (IAHSS), while technical security consultants might choose to join the Construction Specifications Institute (CSI). Consultants who sell to property managers often join groups such as the Building Owners and Managers Association (BOMA) or the International Facility Management Association (IFMA). The list goes on and on.

Most associations operate on a national or international basis but have local branches or chapters in larger cities. For instance, ASIS currently has over 240 chapters worldwide. Association members typically attend local chapter meetings and use these meetings as an opportunity to network with their peers. Educational events are also frequently held at chapter meetings.

Most organizations offer two classes of membership, regular membership, and associate membership. Regular membership is for members which the organization was originally intended to serve, and associate membership is for others allied to the field, including sellers of products and services. For example, in a facilities management organization, people who were facility managers would be regular members, while people who sold products and services to facility managers would be associate members. Most consultants would fall into the associate member category.

Many fledgling security consultants join associations specifically for the purposes of selling their services. They think of chapter meetings as an excellent place to meet potential buyers and close deals. In reality, this is rarely the case. Why?

First of all, the consultant was not the first to think of this strategy. Sellers of nearly every type of product or service also join associations exclusively or primarily for the purpose of selling their wares. Regular members often get overwhelmed at chapter meetings by associate members trying to sell them something. Many regular members can't enjoy themselves at chapter meetings as a result of this constant hounding. To help control this, some associations have imposed limits on the number of associate members that can belong to any one chapter at any given time.

Second, I have found that the people who regularly attend association meetings are not necessarily the ideal buyer of security consulting services. These people are either lower-level employees who can't make buying decisions, or people from companies that are already so squared away that they probably don't need to call in the help of a consultant. My experience has been that the person who is likely to need a consultant may be a member of the association but is probably so busy that they never have the time to attend a chapter meeting.

With that being said, I do think that there is great benefit from joining associations and participating in chapter meetings if you keep the following in mind:

- You can introduce yourself and exchange business cards with influencers and prospects at an association event, but never attempt to make appointments or directly sell your services at an event unless the other person initiates it.
- It is acceptable to enter influencers and prospects met at events into your marketing database and contact them later as a part of your regular marketing campaigns.
- Offer to make presentations on your area of expertise at association events. Most associations are always seeking guest speakers.
- Try to contribute to each association that you belong to in a meaningful way. Consider volunteering on committees and running for elected office at the chapter level.

Civic Organizations

There are a variety of civic organizations such as Rotary International, Lions Club, and Kiwanis, as well as local chambers of commerce in most cities and towns. While these organizations provide many benefits to the community and membership in them can be worthwhile, I don't feel that joining them primarily for the purposes of getting business is very productive.

Although these organizations do provide opportunities for networking, I feel that the chances of meeting someone here that has the need and ability to purchase security consulting services is slim. The membership of these organizations is simply too broad and diverse.

You may achieve different results in your particular specialty or depending on where you are located, but most of us will need to much more specifically target the people who are good prospects for our services.

Public Speaking

Public speaking is an excellent way for an independent security consultant to promote their consulting practice. Over the years, I have spoken to many diverse groups including architects, engineers, construction specifiers, property managers, hospital executives, estate managers, security managers, community crime prevention associations, and many others.

My speaking engagements have taken place in both public forums and within private companies. In almost every case, I have received a paid consulting project as a direct or indirect result of the speaking engagement.

As an example, I spoke to a group of architects on the topic of designing lobbies for good security. At the conclusion of my presentation, an architect approached me and wanted to hire me to help plan security for a government office building she was designing.

In another case, I did a presentation on security for multi-family residential communities at a large property management firm. When the presentation was over, a property manager came up to me and asked me to provide a proposal to conduct an assessment for one of the condominiums that he managed. Since this presentation, I have been asked to speak several additional times at this firm and have ended up doing over 40 separate projects for them – not a bad payback on the time invested.

Here are a few tips on making presentations:

- Make sure your presentations are educational in nature and not just an advertisement for your consulting firm. It's OK to briefly mention your firm and the services that it provides at the end of the presentation.
- Arrive early to get prepared well in advance of your presentation. Be prepared for technical difficulties and have a backup plan.
- Keep presentations short and to the point. It is better to teach one topic well than it is to teach several topics poorly.
- If you use slides, they should be visual aids to support your presentation, never the presentation itself. There is no need to read the text on every slide word by word – this is a sure sign of an amateur presenter.
- The use of images rather than text on slides is preferred. If you must use text, use it sparingly. Big chunky blocks of text are a no-no. Make sure that any text used is easy to read from a distance.
- Minimize the use of animations, sound effects, and flashy transitions between slides. While these can be used once or twice to emphasize a point, excessive use of them can be distracting to your audience.
- A little humor in a presentation can be good, but carefully consider your audience. Something that you think is funny may be offensive to others.
- Make handouts available, but don't pass them out until the end of your presentation. You don't want your audience to

read your handout instead of listening to you while you are giving your talk.

- Leave plenty of time for questions at the end of your session.

Pro Bono Work

"Pro Bono" is a Latin phrase that means "for the public good". In the consulting and legal professions, pro bono work refers to work done for clients at no charge or at a substantially reduced cost.

It is my opinion that every independent security consultant has the obligation to give back to the community by performing at least some pro bono work each year.

I have personally performed pro bono projects for churches, childcare centers, food banks, homeless facilities, and battered women's shelters during my years as a consultant. In each case, the client had a desperate need for my services but had no ability to pay for them. I provided the same level of service to these clients as I did to my paying clients but charged them nothing.

While pro bono projects should never be done exclusively for the purposes of marketing, they do provide indirect marketing benefits. For example, I was hired by a healthcare provider to do a security assessment of their headquarters facility. As it turned out, the president of this organization learned about me through her service on the board of directors of a childcare center that I had done a pro bono project for several years earlier.

Most of my pro bono projects come to me by referral from a past client or influencer. I always ask that the organization requesting pro bono work request it in writing, and that the request be signed by the most senior leader of the organization, typically the president or CEO. I then evaluate each request and decide whether or not to accept the project.

When the project is completed, I request that the pro bono client send me a letter of acknowledgment.

A dilemma faced by many security consultants just starting out is that they have no project references to include in their proposals.

Sometimes, doing a few pro bono projects can be a good way to get some initial references when you are just starting your practice. This can also be a good way to hone your consulting skills prior to starting work on your first paying job.

Articles and Newsletters

Writing magazine articles or publishing your own newsletter or blog can be an excellent way to expose prospects to who you are and what services that you provide. Writing articles allows prospects to get a sense of your knowledge of your specific practice area and can help you to establish a reputation as an expert in your field.

To be effective as a marketing tool, your articles need to be read by potential buyers of your products and services, not just your peers in the security profession. While there is nothing wrong in writing articles directed at your peers, you are in essence "preaching to the choir".

For example, if your market involves selling to facility managers, an article published in the Facilities Management Journal (FMJ) would likely expose you to far more potential buyers than the same article in Security Management magazine would. However, if your primary market is security directors and managers, writing for Security Management might be a good choice.

Newsletters and blogs can be a very effective part of your overall marketing strategy, particularly when used in conjunction with other tools such as email marketing campaigns. However, to be effective, newsletters and blogs need to be frequently updated with new content, a sometimes-daunting task for the busy consultant. Many new consultants ambitiously launch a new newsletter or blog, then fail to keep it up. I think that having a blog where the last update was posted a year or more ago is worse than having no blog at all.

Keep in mind that while writing articles should be part of your long-term marketing strategy, these articles cannot be expected to produce immediate results. Consultants who publish an article and then expect the phone to start ringing the next day are likely to be disappointed.

Social Media

Social media as we know it today didn't exist when I started my consulting practice in 1985. Today, it has become a mainstream method of personal and business communications and is used daily by nearly everyone.

Companies of all sizes are jumping on the social media bandwagon by establishing a presence on LinkedIn, Facebook, Instagram, X (formerly Twitter), and a multitude of other platforms. The use of video and video clips has also become very popular using platforms such as YouTube and TikTok.

Most independent security consultants use social media in one form or another. Some consultants use it only casually and rarely post messages, while other consultants use it very aggressively and post messages nearly every day to tens of thousands of followers.

I have personally been using both X and LinkedIn for over fifteen years and have been posting videos on YouTube for about the same length of time. I find these platforms to be great tools to keep up with what's going on in the industry and to learn about emerging technologies. I also appreciate LinkedIn as a research tool and frequently use it as a source of contacts for my marketing database. I also use LinkedIn and X to notify my followers when I publish a new article on my website.

I would definitely encourage the new consultant to establish a social media presence and use it as one of your marketing tools. For maximum effectiveness, you should post frequently and stay active on your chosen platforms. It is better to participate in only one or two platforms and stay active than it is to subscribe to many platforms and rarely participate in any of them.

As much as I value social media platforms, I don't believe that I have ever gained a project or even an inquiry from a potential client based just on my social media activity. While some of my fellow security consultant colleagues report that they have gotten work directly from their LinkedIn activities, that has not been the case for me.

Based on my personal experience, I would recommend that you not overestimate the effectiveness of social media and definitely not rely on it as your only method of obtaining business. You may find that within your specific practice area, social media works well for you, but it should supplement, not replace, the other marketing techniques outlined in this book.

Podcasts

Podcasts are digital audio programs that are made available on the internet for streaming or downloading. Podcasts are typically released on a scheduled basis, such as every week or every month.

Podcasts can be downloaded through various platforms and apps and can be listened to using a smartphone. Listeners can play podcasts while they are exercising or driving, making them a convenient way to enjoy content while they are engaged in other activities.

Some consultants offer podcasts as a means of promoting their consulting practice and establishing themselves as an expert in their chosen specialty. Podcasts can be an effective form of marketing, particularly once they become popular and you establish a large base of listeners.

You can produce podcasts of an acceptable quality by using equipment and software that you probably already have. However, to produce professional grade podcasts, you will need to make a small investment in a broadcast quality analog microphone, a USB audio interface, and advanced audio editing software.

Before starting a podcast, understand that they require a lot of work. It takes a lot of commitment to produce a new podcast every week or every month, and like with newsletters and blogs, starting something and then failing to keep it up can send the wrong message to your audience.

Advertising

The new consultant will be presented with numerous opportunities to purchase advertising of all types, including newspaper and magazine ads, and ads on social media sites. You may also be approached to get a booth at a trade show or to sponsor an industry luncheon or other event.

Over the years I have been in business, I have tried nearly every advertising option available and have found most to be completely worthless in terms of generating new business for my security consulting business. I very much wish that I could just place an ad somewhere and have projects start rolling in, but in our business, this just doesn't happen – at least not for me. That is why I have developed the many other marketing techniques described elsewhere in this book.

I have asked other successful security consultants about some of the biggest mistakes that they made when starting their consulting practice and one of the answers is almost always *"spending money on advertising that didn't work"*.

I continue to experiment with new types of advertising, and occasionally purchase ads to support charitable organizations that I am involved with, but don't consider advertising of any type to be a serious part of my marketing strategy.

I would encourage you to do your own experimenting with advertising but use caution. Be careful not to spend money that you cannot afford to lose on advertising that is unlikely to produce results.

Pay Per Click Advertising

A particularly dangerous form of advertising is the "pay per click" advertising offered by the major search engines, including Google AdWords and Microsoft Advertising (Bing Ads). These services allow advertisers to bid for paid ads that come up when a user enters a specified keyword or phrase in the search engine. These ads display at the top of the page above the regular search results. When the user clicks on the ad, they are automatically linked to the web page of the advertiser.

For example, let's say a user enters the search term "security consultant" in Google. This will bring up a list of regular search results, plus a handful of paid ads at the top of the page. If the user clicks on one of the ads, the user is directed to the advertiser's web page and is automatically charged an advertising fee by Google. Because the advertiser is only charged when a user clicks the ad, this is known as "pay per click" advertising.

Because there are only a limited number of spaces available for paid ads, advertisers bid against one another for placement. The higher the bid, the greater the chance that the advertiser's ad will appear on the top of the first page of search results. The ads of advertisers bidding less appear lower on the page, or don't show up until the second or third page of search results.

Bids are set by the advertiser in advance for each keyword or phrase. For instance, a bidder might agree to pay $1 per click when the phrase "security consultant" was used, but $3 per click when the phrase "security assessment" was used.

Naturally, every advertiser wants to appear on the first page, so bidding wars frequently occur, driving up the amount paid per click. This can result in some unbelievably high costs per click. For example, the phrase "security vulnerability assessment" on Google currently costs in excess of $13 per click in my market area. Certain keywords in the security consulting profession can cost $25 or more per click.

Advertisers can end up quickly spending thousands of dollars a month on pay per click advertising and have very little to show for it. The bidding process can bring out the gambling instinct in some advertisers, causing them to continually increase the amount that they pay per click, being certain that the next big "win" is just around the corner.

It should be kept in mind that only a small percentage of clicks may result in an actual inquiry from a client. People looking for employment, conducting research, or simply amusing themselves may click your ad, and you pay for it whether it results in actual business or not. I strongly urge all security consultants who are considering the use of pay per click advertising to proceed with extreme caution.

Directory Listings

There are numerous directories where the security consultant can be listed as a provider of consulting services in their specialty. These directories are published by various trade organizations in the security, legal, and healthcare professions, as well as organizations that represent industries such as property management, cannabis, gaming, and many others.

The majority of these directories are now offered online, although a few organizations still continue to produce printed directories. While some organizations offer free listings to their members, some require the payment of a fee to get a listing. Most directories also offer the opportunity to purchase expanded listings or display ads.

I have obtained both free and paid listings in various types of directories over the years, but like with other types of advertising, I have never received business as a result of a directory listing. Other security consultants that I have spoken with have reported similar results.

One notable exception is forensic consultants, who report that having a listing or ad in one or more of the directories used by lawyers to find experts is essential, especially when just getting started in forensic work. Once they have established a reputation and start getting referrals from other lawyers, the directory listing becomes less important.

Not all forensic directories are the same. You should do research to determine which ones might work best in your particular region or area of practice. Two widely used directories are the JurisPro Expert Witness Directory and the SEAK Expert Witness Directory.

Paid Articles and Awards

Some publications will contact the consultant and say that they are writing a feature article about them. To get this article published and to obtain reprints of it for promotional purposes, the consultant must make a payment to the publication.

Consultants are also sometimes contacted by an organization that claims that they have been chosen to win an award, or to be included in a "Who's-Who" list of leading consultants in their specialty. In order to receive these honors, they must pay a fee.

In most cases, these offers are a complete scam. Most reputable organizations don't require recipients of an award to pay a fee, and while a legitimate publication may charge a fee for reprints, there is never a fee to get an article published. Nonetheless, some consultants, either out of ego or ignorance, will fall for them.

Promotional Products

Some consultants have promotional items that they give away to clients, potential clients, and influencers. These items can include pens, paperweights, key chains, flashlights, coffee mugs, hats, and a wide variety of other products. The products usually include the consultant's logo and name and may also include a telephone number and other contact information. The intended goal of these products is to keep the consultant's name in front of potential clients and influencers.

I have personally not used promotional products as a part of my marketing program but have received numerous promotional items from other consultants and suppliers of security products. In most cases, the item that I am receiving is of little value to me and it quickly gets disposed of. The last thing I need is another cheap pen or key chain that I will never use.

In rare cases, I receive something that I find worth keeping. An example is a cell phone stand that I received from another well-known security consultant. I find this stand to be extremely helpful and it sits in a prominent location on my desk, reminding me of this consultant every day.

If you do choose to use promotional products for marketing, I would suggest that they be unique, of high-quality, and likely to be used by the people who receive them. I think that it is far better to give out a smaller quantity of more expensive items that are likely to be kept than it is to give away mass quantities of inexpensive items that are likely to be thrown away.

Trade Show Booths

Many organizations put on trade shows at the national, regional, or local level. In many cases, they offer the opportunity for sponsors to purchase booths at these shows. While most sponsors are sellers of products, providers of services such as security consulting can also purchase a booth.

The cost of trade show booths varies dramatically, with the cost of a booth at some national shows ranging between $25,000 and

$100,000 or more. The cost of a booth at a regional or local show typically ranges between $500 and $5,000 depending on the size of the event. In addition to the cost of the booth, there are often extra charges to rent the chairs and tables and to obtain internet service.

My only experience with trade show booths is at the national level during the short time that I was working for a large international risk consulting firm. During the days that I staffed the booth, there were few people stopping by the booth, and the ones that did stop were usually just friends or industry colleagues stopping by to say "Hi". We also got quite a few visits from other vendors at the show wanting to sell us something.

Over the three days of the event, we may have obtained three or four legitimate leads, definitely not worth the cost of renting the booth and paying for the time and travel costs necessary for our employees to staff it.

The lower costs of the smaller regional and local shows may make them affordable to some consultants, but I would definitely weigh the costs against the benefits. In some specialties, a booth at the right trade show may make sense, but I suspect that for most of us, there are better, more cost-effective ways to reach potential clients.

Sales Strategies

Many new consultants stop selling when they get a project and only resume selling when that project is completed. They also usually work on projects sequentially, completing one project before they start another. This results in an erratic flow of income throughout the year and the start and stop nature of their sales efforts produces inconsistent results. I call this strategy the "Sell-Work-Sell" Sales Model.

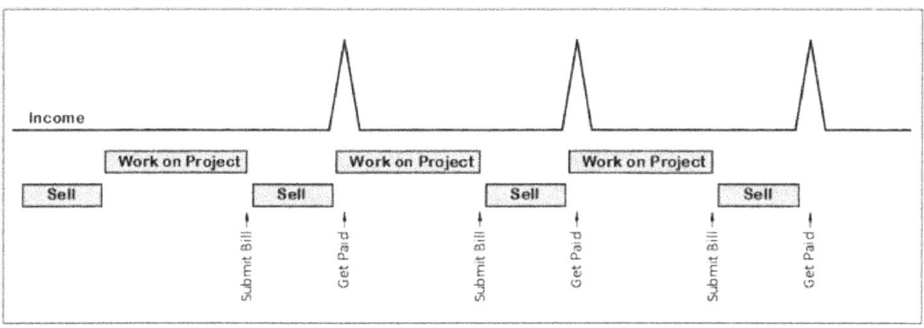

Sell-Work-Sell Sales Model

A far better approach is to sell continuously throughout the year and to have overlapping projects. I call this the "Constantly Selling Sales Model". While income in the consulting business is always unpredictable, this model provides a more balanced revenue stream that more closely matches your expenses. This model also provides greater consistency in your sales efforts which produces better results

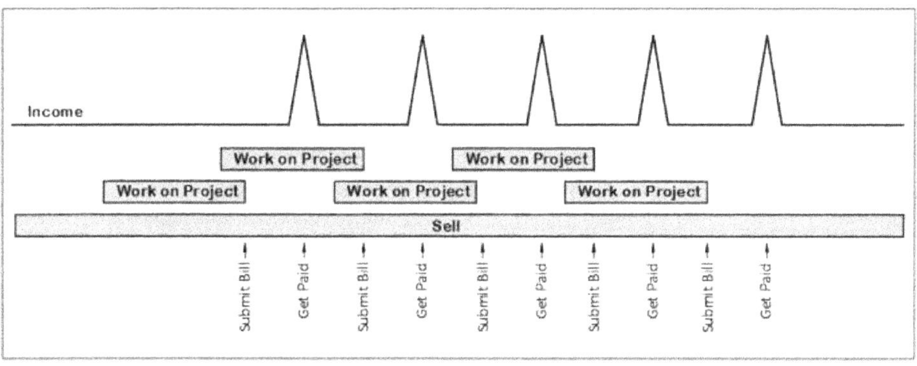

Constantly Selling Sales Model

Chapter 9 - Proposal Writing

Proposal writing is an important part of the security consulting profession, and almost every consultant will be required to write proposals on a frequent basis. Within this chapter, I will discuss how to write informal proposals and how to prepare formal proposals in response to a Request for Proposals (RFP). We will also discuss a close relative of the RFP, the Request for Qualifications (RFQ).

Purpose of Proposals

A proposal is a written offer between the security consultant and the prospective client. Proposals spell out in detail what services the consultant intends to provide, the time that it will take to deliver them, and what they will cost. Most proposals also include language specifying the terms and conditions under which the consultant will work, such as how payment will be made or what types of expenses will be reimbursed.

Proposals are one of the final steps in the marketing process and one of the most important. The primary purpose of all of your sales and marketing efforts thus far have been to put you in a position to submit a proposal to the prospective client. When accepted by the client, the proposal becomes the basis for the written contract for consulting services under which you will provide your work.

Types of Proposals

There are two types of proposals commonly prepared by the independent security consultant.

The first type of proposal is the "informal proposal". Informal proposals are typically prepared as the outcome of an in-person sales call or telephone conversation with a prospective client. During your conversations with the client, you verbally came to an agreement as to what type of services were needed. A proposal is drafted to confirm in writing the exact scope of the work that is to be provided, what the services will cost, and how long it will take to perform them. Because the consultant usually has wide latitude in how this type of proposal can be prepared, I call proposals of this type "informal proposals". Clients often call proposals of this type "bids", "estimates" or "quotes" and will sometimes use one of these terms when requesting a proposal. For example: *"Please send me a quote to conduct a security assessment of my building"*.

The second type of proposal is the "formal proposal". Formal proposals are prepared in response to a formal written request issued by a prospective client. The requests are known as "Request-for-Proposals" or "RFPs". RFPs are commonly used by larger companies and government agencies when requesting security consulting services. Proposals prepared in response to RFPs must usually follow a specific format prescribed by the client and are often considerably more elaborate than an informal proposal.

Informal Proposals

Informal proposals are the type most frequently prepared by most independent security consultants. If your marketing efforts have been successful, you will be preparing many informal proposals every year. It is important to have a system in place that allows you to quickly and efficiently prepare informal proposals.

Before getting into the specifics of preparing an informal proposal, it is imperative that you understand that proposals of this type are not merely a statement of tasks to be performed and fees but are a powerful selling tool. Prospective clients often make purchasing decisions based solely on what they see in your proposal. You should use every opportunity within the proposal to convince the client that you are the right consultant for the job.

There is wide variation in the way that independent security consultants prepare their informal proposals. Many consultants prepare their proposals in letter format, using their letterhead as the first page. Proposals prepared in this manner are often called "letter proposals". Other consultants prepare their proposals somewhat like a report, with a front cover, back cover, table of contents, and perhaps several appendixes. My preferred format is the letter proposal, and I use this format on about 90% of the proposals that I produce.

Regardless of format used, every informal proposal should include at least the following sections:

Opening Statement

Within this section, thank the client for giving you the opportunity to submit a proposal, and briefly recap any prior meetings or conversations in which you obtained the information that is used as the basis for this proposal.

Introduction

Within this section, provide a brief overview of your consulting firm, your credentials and experience, and relevant projects that you have completed. If you can, provide the names of one or two notable clients that you have worked for, preferably in the same industry as the company that you are submitting the proposal to. Keep this section brief – you will have the opportunity to expand on your qualifications later.

Background

Within this section, provide a brief overview of the client's business, facility locations, and the conditions that caused the client to seek the services of a security consultant. The purpose of this section is to demonstrate to the client that you completely understand their situation and the reasons they need your expertise.

Statement of Requirements

Within this section, you will drill down on the client's problems or requirements in greater detail. Provide a narrative that shows that you have an in-depth understanding of the problems that the client is trying to solve and the results that the client wishes to achieve.

In the case of a security management consultant, the client's problem might be shrinkage in the warehouse or threats of violence against employees. In the case of a technical security consultant, the client's problem may be that their video surveillance system is outdated and no longer produces the quality of recorded images that are desired.

Proposed Solution

Within this section, you explain in detail how you intend to help the client to solve the problem or meet the requirements that were described in the previous section.

In the case of a security management consultant, the proposed solution might be to conduct a security assessment or to develop a workplace violence training program for employees. In the case of a technical security consultant, the proposed solution might be to conduct a study that determines the feasibility of replacing the client's existing security system, or to prepare design drawings and specifications for security system replacement.

Scope of Work

Within this section, you provide a list of the specific tasks involved in implementing the solutions that you have proposed in the previous section. This is normally a numbered or bulleted list that shows the tasks that the consultant intends to perform from start to finish. If the project will have multiple phases, you would indicate this here and provide details on what's included in each phase.

Project Team

Within this section, identify the specific consultants and other team members who will be assigned to work on this project. If you are a one-person consulting firm and performing the project without the use of associates, the "project team" would be you.

Provide information on your qualifications and experience, specifically as they relate to the scope of work outlined in the previous section. If possible, give actual examples of where you have previously performed a similar scope of work for other clients. If you have never done anything exactly like this before, explain how your experience in other areas can be directly applied to this scope of work.

Consultants who are just starting out and don't have any actual consulting project experience should refer to any relevant experience gained while working for previous employers.

Remember, only qualifications and experience directly applicable to the project being proposed should be listed here – other experience should be listed in your resume at the back of the proposal.

Client References

Within this section, provide a listing of previous clients for whom you have worked, preferably ones who had projects similar to the one currently being proposed. Client references should include:

- Client name.
- Project location.
- Name of contact person.
- Contact person's email address and telephone number.
- Brief summary of services that you provided on this project.

New consultants without previous project experience may wish to use contacts from previous employers as references. For example, if you were previously a corporate security manager and provided security consultation to your distribution centers, you may wish to use one or more of the distribution center managers that you worked with as references.

Fees and Expenses

Within this section, specify what and how you will charge the client for the services outlined in your scope of work. Determine how you will charge using one of the methods described in Chapter 7. The most commonly used methods are the "Straight Hourly with Not-to-Exceed Amount" method and the "Fixed-Fee Amount Method"

Determining the number of hours that will be required to perform a consulting assignment is as much of an art as it is a science. It is particularly difficult to do this when you are just starting out because you have no actual experience to base your estimates on. After you get a few consulting projects under your belt, you will find it easier to make more accurate estimates.

When preparing an estimate, a good place to start is the itemized list of tasks outlined in the Scope of Work. Go through each task and identify the amount of time that you think will be required to perform each task. Total up the amount of time required for all tasks and use this as the starting point for your estimate. Add time for preparation, travel, research, and any other activities directly attributable to the project.

After the total hours have been determined, calculate your fixed-fee amount or not-to-exceed amount by multiplying your total hours by your hourly billing rate. Also specify which project expenses are to be reimbursed by the client and how they will be paid. If possible, provide an approximate estimate of what the total expenses will be.

If you are asking for a retainer payment in advance, specify the amount of the retainer here.

<u>Schedule</u>

Within this section, provide an estimate of the total time that you think will be required to complete the project. Use the total number of hours estimated in the previous section as a starting point to determine the total number of days that will be required. Allow time in your schedule to conduct research, obtain information from others, and make follow-up trips to the project site if needed. Also factor in any holidays or days where you are unavailable into your estimate.

Keep in mind that as an independent consultant, you can't afford to drop everything and work full time on any single project – you need to make gaps in your schedule to work on other client's projects and to handle your administrative and marketing activities.

When estimating a completion date, assume that some things will go wrong and that it will take longer than expected rather than the other way around. It is better to deliver a project a little earlier than promised than it is to miss a deadline and be late.

Once you have determined your schedule, specify it within your proposal. For simple projects this can just be a statement of estimated completion time in calendar days. ("Estimated completion time for this project is 30 calendar days"). For more complicated projects, you may wish to use a chart or graph to graphically illustrate your proposed schedule.

Also indicate within this section the time that you require between the day that the client accepts the proposal and the day when you are available to start work. ("XYZ Consultants would be available to start work on this project within 15 calendar days of acceptance of this proposal").

Terms and Conditions

Some consultants have a standard Professional Services Agreement that they attach to their proposal. This agreement includes contract language with the terms and conditions under which the consultant will work when performing the project. When the client decides to accept the consultant's proposal, they sign the Professional Services Agreement and return it to the consultant.

Other consultants include terms and conditions within the body of their proposal, allowing the proposal itself to serve as the contract for consulting services when signed by the client.

Terms and conditions found in Professional Services Agreements and within proposals often include:

- Payment terms.
- Insurance requirements.
- Indemnification provisions.
- Confidentiality requirements.
- Working conditions.
- Ownership of work product.
- Type and quantity of deliverables.
- Contract termination.
- Governing laws.
- Disclaimers and limits of liability.

It is recommended that your legal advisor draft any Professional Services Agreement that you intend to use, as well as provide standard terms and conditions that you can include in your proposals. Any contract language concerning insurance or indemnification should also be reviewed by your insurance broker to assure that your agreements are consistent with your insurance coverage.

Some consultants choose to write their own legal agreements using information found in books or on the internet. I discourage security consultants from trying to act as their own attorney and strongly recommend that a competent professional be hired to draft all legal documents. Keep in mind that, once a standard agreement or standard terms and conditions are drafted, they can be reused on most future projects, so the costs of legal fees are a one-time expense.

<u>Closing Statement</u>

This section closes out the proposal and typically includes a final thank you to the client, and the name, title, signature and telephone number of the person preparing the proposal.

<u>Acceptance</u>

If the proposal will also be used as the contract for consulting services, an acceptance block should be provided just below the closing statement. This acceptance block should indicate that by signing below, the client accepts the proposal as written. A place for client name, authorized representative name, signature, and date should also be provided.

<u>Appendices</u>

Appendices are attachments to the proposal that provide additional information. Appendices can typically include:

- Resumes of team members.
- Complete listing of clients and completed projects.
- Firm brochure.
- Letters of recommendations from past clients.

- Copies of licenses, awards and certifications.

Formal Proposals and RFPs

Formal proposals are those prepared in response to request-for-proposals (RFPs) issued by larger companies and government agencies seeking consulting services. In some cases, RFPs are initiated solely by the client without having any previous contact with the consultants who are being asked to respond to them. In other cases, the client may have previously called in one or more consultants prior to writing the RFP as a means to learn more about what services are available and how they should be specified.

The RFP process varies from company to company and agency to agency, but the process can include up to ten steps. Here is a summary of the steps in sequential order:

#1 - Initial Contact with Proposers

During this step, the client identifies potentially qualified consultants and notifies them of the upcoming RFP. In some cases, a client representative will speak personally with each consultant to briefly confirm that they are indeed interested and eligible to participate in the RFP process. Some clients at this point will require that the consultant sign a non-disclosure agreement (NDA) in order to participate further.

#2 - Issuance of Formal RFP

During this step, the RFP itself is issued. The RFP includes a description of the desired scope of work, locations where work will be performed, the timeline in which the client hopes to accomplish the work, and the work products that the consultant is expected to deliver.

The RFP will also provide specific instructions on how the consultant's proposal is to be formatted and what information is to be included. Most RFPs also include a sample of the agreement that the consultant will be expected to sign if awarded the job, as well as numerous forms that need to be filled out and submitted with the proposal. Most RFPs also include a statement of the criteria that will be used to score the proposals. This typically involves the use of a point system where points are awarded based on the proposer's qualifications, previous experience, project approach, price, and other such factors.

#3 - Preproposal Conference

In most cases, the client will hold a preproposal conference shortly after the RFP is issued. The purpose of this conference is to verbally explain the RFP requirements to potential proposers and give them an opportunity to ask questions. Proposers may also be given a tour of the client's facilities so that they can see where the requested work will be performed.

The proposer's attendance at preproposal conferences can be optional or mandatory. If attendance is optional, proposers can decide for themselves if they want to attend. If attendance is mandatory, the proposer must attend in order to be eligible to submit a proposal.

Attending the preproposal conference is a great way to gauge the level of interest in the project and to find out which other consultants may be competing for the job. Many consultants also use these conferences as an opportunity to meet other consultants and explore possible partnering arrangements. There is usually a written sign-in sheet at preproposal conferences. Most clients are happy to provide a copy of this sheet to all attendees to allow them to get in touch with one another for the purpose of partnering.

#4 - Deadline for Questions

Most clients require that all questions that proposers have about the RFP be submitted in writing. The exception is the questions asked at the preproposal conference, which are taken down in writing by a client representative. The process allows for questions to be submitted up until an established cut-off date. After this date, no more questions will be accepted.

The answers to all questions are answered by the client in writing and are distributed to all proposers at the same time.

#5 - Issuance of Addendums

The client will typically issue one or more addendums to the RFP during the course of the RFP process. Addendums are used to provide answers to any questions asked by proposers and to correct any mistakes or misunderstandings discovered in the RFP.

The goal is to provide all proposers with the same information. If one proposer asks a question, both the question and the answer are sent to all proposers in the form of an addendum.

The last addendum is typically issued at least seven days prior to the proposal due date. Proposers are required to acknowledge receipt of all addendums in their proposal or by other means.

#6 - Proposal Due Date

The RFP will establish a firm date and time by which all proposals must be received. It is the responsibility of the proposer to see that the proposal arrives by the established deadline, regardless of the delivery method used. Most clients will not consider proposals received after the deadline, regardless of the circumstances that caused the delay.

#7 - Proposal Opening and Scoring

After the proposals are received, they are opened and evaluated by the client. This is usually done in private, but sometimes a public agency may hold a meeting where proposals are opened publicly. The client will typically use a selection committee to evaluate and score each proposal. The selection committee is usually made up of between three and five employees who have a stake in the outcome of the consulting project, as well as one or more members of the client's purchasing department

The first step in the evaluation process is to determine whether or not the proposer fully complied with all requirements stated in the RFP. If so, the proposal is deemed to be "responsive" and is set aside for further evaluation.

If a proposer has left required information out of their proposal or has not fully complied with the instructions in the RFP, their proposal is deemed to be "non-responsive". Non-responsive proposals are almost always disqualified immediately and not subjected to any type of further evaluation.

All responsive proposals are then evaluated by the selection committee using the scoring criteria that was stated in the RFP. Points are awarded in each category and totaled up to give each proposal a numeric score.

In some cases, the selection committee has the authority to immediately award the contract to the highest scoring proposer. In other cases, the process may require additional evaluation of the highest-ranking firms before a final selection is made.

Typically, the top three highest ranking proposers are chosen for further evaluation. The list of the top scoring proposers is often called the "short-list", and the consultants on this list are often known as the "short-listed" firms.

#8 - Announcement of Short-Listed Firms

After the short-list has been created, all proposers are usually notified by the client. Proposers not on the short-list usually know that this is the end of the line for them and that there is likely no chance that they will be awarded the contract. Proposers who are on the short-list know that they are still under consideration for the project and should be prepared to be interviewed.

#9 - Interviews with Short-Listed Firms

The short-listed firms are asked to come in and make a presentation to the selection committee. Committee members have the opportunity to ask questions and get a better feel for the consulting team and how they operate. Short-listed firms may also be asked to bring examples of previous work to the interview.

#10 - Final Selection and Contract Award

The selection committee makes a final selection of a consultant based on the interviews with the short-listed firms. The client's purchasing department begins the process to award the contract to the chosen firm. The short-listed firms that were not chosen are notified.

As you can see, the RFP process can be long and complicated, and the chance that you will be awarded a contract at the end of the process is far from certain. Nonetheless, security consultants selling services to certain types of clients may need to frequently participate in the RFP process in order to obtain a majority of their work. Consultants serving other types of clients may rarely need to respond to RFPs but should be prepared to do so if the right opportunity arises.

Responding to an RFP and preparing a formal proposal can require a serious investment of time and energy. Before deciding to respond, you need to make a realistic assessment of your chances of winning the project. Some questions to be asked include:

- How closely do my qualifications and experience match those being sought in the RFP?
- How many actual projects of a similar type have I actually performed?
- Can I meet the insurance, financial, and other requirements in the RFP?
- What is the potential value of this contract in terms of dollars?
- Is the work located in places that I can serve in a cost-effective manner?
- Do I have the resources necessary to perform a project of this type and size?
- Is the size of my consulting firm a good match for the project, or would the client likely prefer to work with a larger company?
- How many other consulting firms are likely to be competing for the same project? How do their qualifications and experience compare to my own?
- Does the client have an existing relationship with another consultant, or does it appear that another consultant is already preferred by the client?

Once you have made the decision to respond to an RFP, it is suggested that you take the following steps:

a) Completely read the RFP in its entirety from cover to cover. Read thoroughly – don't skim. Highlight items that you think are significant. Note any limitations on proposal length that the client may have specified.

b) Completely read the RFP again, but this time, as you go along, create a checklist of every item that the client has requested that you include in your proposal.

c) If the RFP requires that proposals be submitted in a specific format, create an outline of this format. This outline would typically include separate sections for things such as qualifications, project experience, project team, project approach, proposed fees, etc., arranged in the order that the client prefers them.

d) If the RFP does not specify a proposal format, use your own format similar to the one that you use in your informal proposals.

e) Begin to prepare your proposal. Using your outline, begin to fill in the information under each section. Look at your checklist as you go along to identify items that should be included in each section. Gradually work on all sections until the first draft of your proposal is complete.

f) Fill out all forms as requested in the RFP. Provide any requested attachments that the client may have specified (resumes, certificates of insurances, copies of licenses, etc.)

g) When your draft proposal including all forms and attachments is complete, go through your checklist again to make sure that all requested items have been provided. Be sure that the number of pages in your proposal doesn't exceed any limits that were stated by the client.

h) Carefully proofread your proposal, and if possible, have a second and third person proofread it as well. The more eyes that examine a document, the better the chances that mistakes will be caught.

i) Make any final changes that are needed and prepare your proposal for submission to the client. RFPs usually provide specific instructions on how many copies of the proposal are to be provided and how it is to be printed and bound. Many clients today may also request that an electronic copy of the proposal be provided in addition to (or in place of) the printed copies.

j) Submit your proposal prior to the specified deadline. If possible, deliver your proposal using a method that provides proof of delivery.

Here are some additional thoughts on the RFP and formal proposal process:

- Make the decision early as to whether or not to respond to a formal RFP to allow ample time to prepare the proposal. Don't wait until the last minute to get started.
- Keep the materials that you will likely need when preparing proposals readily available at all times. This can include previously prepared descriptions of your qualifications and experience, project narratives, references, letters of recommendation, resumes, and copies of licenses and certifications. Having this information on hand can keep you from scrambling to find it at the last minute.
- When using previously prepared materials or copying and pasting from old proposals, be sure that all information is completely relevant to the current proposal. Don't sacrifice the quality of your proposal by using outdated or inappropriate materials just to save time. Be especially careful to check that names, places, and dates are accurate. It is extremely embarrassing to have a sentence pasted-in from a previous proposal that says something like "*We are excited to have this opportunity to work for the SBC Company*" when the proposal is actually being submitted to a different company.

- A surprising number of proposals are rejected or poorly scored because they don't clearly address the requirements stated in the RFP. This is because many proposers assume that they know what the client needs better than they do. They prepare their proposal based on their preconceptions – rather than what is written in the RFP. Read the RFP carefully and assume that the client wants everything that they say they want, even if you think that you know better.
- Prepare and submit your proposal exactly as instructed in the RFP. If you have an alternative project approach that is better, cheaper, or faster, ask the client for permission to include an explanation of this approach in a separate attachment to the proposal. Never propose alternative approaches within the main body of the proposal.
- Unless specifically prohibited by the instructions, make use of photos, charts, and other graphics within your proposal when they can help you to better communicate your message.
- Have all requirements in the RFP concerning insurance coverage and indemnification reviewed by your insurance broker before submitting the proposal. You don't want to agree to provide something that your insurance won't cover.
- If there are any requirements that you can't or don't wish to comply with, ask the client about these in advance. For example, many RFPs will request detailed personal financial information, something that some consultants refuse to provide. If you ask in advance you may get the requirement waived, but if you simply leave it out of your proposal without asking, your proposal may be disqualified.
- If you are an out-of-town consultant competing against local consulting firms, you are most often operating at a serious disadvantage. If you choose to go forward despite this disadvantage, have a strategy in place to explain why your lack of a local office will not be a problem and why it will not increase costs to the client. Clearly explain your strategy in your proposal in advance – don't try to avoid the issue.

- When attending the preproposal conference, pay close attention to conversations between the client representatives and other consultants in the room. If a client asks one of the other consultants in the room something along the lines of "*Bob, how was your fishing trip last weekend?*" it could be a clue that there is some type of previous relationship.
- If you have strong qualifications in most areas of skill that the RFP is requesting, but are lacking in a few areas, consider forming a partnering arrangement with one or more other consultants. Also consider a partnering arrangement when the project may be too big for you to handle alone or is spread out over a large geographical area. (More on partnering arrangements in Chapter 14.)
- For technical security projects, you will often find that the client has a preferred engineering firm that they use for the majority of their electrical and mechanical design work. A representative of this firm will very likely show up at the preproposal conference, even if their firm lacks security design experience. If you partner with this firm, the client gains the benefit of your security expertise, plus the comfort of working with someone that they already trust – often a winning combination.
- In rare cases, the RFP process may be rigged from the start – the client already has a security consultant that they want to work with and are going through the RFP process just as a formality. During the evaluation process, they will score proposals in such a way that their preferred firm is the winner. This is not fair, and probably not legal, but a fact of life, nonetheless. Don't let the fact that this occasionally occurs discourage you from submitting proposals on projects that you are qualified to perform.
- Some clients prefer a larger "big-name" national consulting firm over a sole practitioner or a small team of consultants. This is often true when the evaluation committee of a large corporation or government entity wants to make what they feel is a safe and reliable purchasing decision that would be difficult

for their bosses to criticize if something went wrong. If you or your team have already worked for other large well-known organizations, you may be able to overcome this mindset, but in some cases, smaller consulting firms simply have no chance of winning in this situation.

Request-for-Qualifications (RFQ)

In years past, it was considered unethical for the providers of professional services to compete on the basis of price. It was expected that one would choose their doctor, lawyer or architect on the basis of qualifications, not on how cheaply they would work. During this era, it was considered taboo to ask a professional to submit a bid or proposal based on price.

Today, this prohibition has largely disappeared. Professionals of all types regularly compete based on price. However, some companies and government agencies still see the value in selecting their professionals based on qualifications and not just price alone. To achieve this, these purchasers divide their evaluation process into two separate parts, one to evaluate the proposer's qualifications, and the other to evaluate the proposer's price.

In some cases, this is done as a part of the RFP process described above. Proposers are asked to split their proposals into two parts, one part that contains the proposer's price, and the other part that contains everything else. The part that contains the price is placed in a sealed envelope. The selection committee scores the proposals and selects three finalists based on qualifications. The envelopes of the three finalists are then opened to see who is the lowest priced. In some cases, the finalist who has the lowest price wins. In other cases, the merits of each of the finalists are weighed against their price. A final selection is then made based on who the committee feels will provide the most overall value.

Many government agencies are required by law to use a qualifications-based selection process to choose certain professionals such as architects, engineers, and consultants. These agencies use a process called the Request for Qualifications (RFQ) process. The RFQ is a close relative to the RFP but focuses exclusively on the qualifications of the proposer. An RFQ typically does not ask for the consultant's proposed scope of work, project approach, or how much the consultant will charge.

The RFQ process is similar to the RFP process and may follow some or all of the same steps. However, selection of the finalist is made solely on the basis of qualifications – price is never discussed. Once a finalist is chosen, the client then sits down with the chosen firm to negotiate a scope of work, price and schedule. In most cases, the finalist will be awarded the contract at the end of the negotiations.

In some cases, the client and the finalist may find themselves unable to reach mutually agreeable terms. In these cases, the client may terminate negotiations with the finalist and start negotiations with the second highest scoring finalist. If an agreement cannot be reached with the second finalist, the client moves to the third finalist, and so on, until a satisfactory agreement is reached, or the client decides to abandon the process and start over.

When preparing a response to an RFQ, the consultant submits a "Statement of Qualifications" (SOQ) rather than a proposal. The steps used to prepare a SOQ are nearly identical to the steps used to prepare a formal proposal described above, except that all information unrelated to qualifications is usually omitted.

The RFQ process is used primarily by government agencies, but in some cases, private companies may choose to use this process also.

Chapter 10 - Selling to Government Agencies

Government agencies are major purchasers of security consulting services. Nearly every type of security consultant will have the opportunity at some point to sell services to government agencies, and some consultants will do all or a majority of their business with government entities.

There are considerable differences between doing business with a government agency and doing business with a corporation or privately-owned company. Within this chapter, I will explain some of these differences and provide some guidelines for successfully working with government agencies.

Who Are Government Agencies?

The term "government agency" as I use it in this book refers to city, county, and state governments, as well as semi-governmental entities such as school districts, libraries, hospital districts, housing authorities, public utilities, and many other such agencies operated for the public good.

Government agencies also include the federal government and all of its branches, but within this book, I will not provide specific details on working with the federal government. Consultants who desire more information on this topic are urged to contact the General Services Administration (GSA) and the Small Business Administration (SBA). Both of these organizations offer extensive resources to people who wish to sell to the federal government.

Why Are Government Agencies Different?

Most government agencies are supported directly through taxes paid by taxpayers, or indirectly through license fees, surcharges, fines, and other charges imposed on the public. When government agencies spend money on products or services, they are spending the public's money. As a result, there are specific laws on how these products and services must be procured.

The specific laws on government agency procurement vary from agency to agency, but most revolve around the following basic principles:

- The procurement process must be fair and accessible to all qualified providers of products and services.
- All qualified suppliers must be given an equal opportunity to compete. Arbitrary selections of suppliers by the agency cannot be made.
- The procurement process must be transparent to the public.
- Preferential treatment may be given to groups that have been historically excluded or underrepresented based on race, gender, economic circumstances, and other factors.
- Reasonable prices shall be paid for products and services. The agency has the right to determine how the supplier arrives at their prices and may place limits on the level of profit that the supplier can make.

How Government Agencies Buy

Government agencies must follow a specific set of guidelines when procuring products and services. These guidelines establish different rules depending on the amount of money being spent. For example, a government agency might have the following rules:

- $5,000 or less: an agency can purchase any needed product or service without following any type of competitive procurement process.
- $5,001 to $15,000: The agency must get informal proposals or quotes from three suppliers. The supplier with the lowest cost must be chosen. There is no requirement to publicly advertise the procurement to the public.
- $15,001 and up: The agency must use a formal RFP process and publicly advertise the opportunity.

There are often policies that allow exceptions to the rules stated above to be made. One exception is what are known as "sole source" items. These are items available only from a single supplier or service provider. For example, a replacement part for a specific type of equipment may only be available from the original equipment manufacturer. This would make the part a sole source item and exempt from normal purchasing rules.

Sole source services are less common but do occasionally come up. For example, a certain type of specialized training may be available exclusively from a single consulting firm in the country. Because there are no other sources of this training, it would be considered a sole source service. The agency could contract with the consulting firm for this service without having to go through a competitive procurement process.

Some procurement policies require that sole source purchases be publicly advertised when they exceed a certain dollar amount, say $10,000. If the contract for the specialized training described above was $35,000, the agency would be required to advertise a "Notice of Intent to Award a Sole Source". This notice tells the public that the agency is about to award a sole source contract for training to the consulting company. The notice gives other possible suppliers an opportunity to challenge the sole source procurement by submitting proof that they can provide equal or better services. It is usually within the discretion of the agency to decide whether to act on the challenge or not. Challenges of this type are rarely successful.

Most agencies also have policies that allow products or services to be purchased without following procurement rules in cases of emergency. For example, if a water main broke and had to be immediately repaired, the agency would usually be permitted to hire a contractor to repair the damage without going through the competitive bid process.

The final exception that permits agencies to get around procurement rules is a specific service provider's previous experience in working with the agency. The theory is that an existing service provider is already familiar with the agency's needs and can therefore provide services more expeditiously and less expensively than a new service provider could. For example, an electrical engineer who previously worked on a building might already be intimately familiar with its power distribution system. This engineer would have the ability to design additions to this system much more efficiently than a new engineer, who would have a steep learning curve before beginning the design work.

This latter exception is the one that is the most contentious because in theory, it allows a single service provider to get entrenched in a particular agency, and other service providers are never given an opportunity to compete for the work. Nonetheless, this exception is frequently used to justify the sole source procurement of certain types of services.

How Does This Apply to Security Consultants?

Most security consulting projects will be of a size that exceeds the discretionary spending limits of most government agencies. For example, if a security assessment of a city building cost $15,000 and the agency's limit was $10,000, the project would most likely have to go out to bid using an RFP or RFQ process.

Some agencies like to play tricks such as asking the consultant to make sure that their estimate comes in just under the limit, or by splitting a larger project into several smaller projects and awarding each separately.

But for the most part, security consultants who want to work for government agencies should expect to go through the RFP or RFQ process in order to get the work.

Learning about Opportunities

Government agencies are required to provide public notice of any RFPs or RFQs for security consulting services that they intend to issue. How does the security consultant learn about opportunities of this type, especially when there may be hundreds of government agencies within the consultant's chosen market area? Here are the ways that consultants most often learn about opportunities:

Registering with Individual Agencies

Most government agencies operate websites specifically designed to help them buy products and services. Consultants are given the opportunity to register as vendors on these websites. When registering, they specify the categories of services that they are capable of providing. When the agency needs a product or service, an email notice is automatically sent to the vendors who have registered in the appropriate categories. Most RFPs and RFQs for consulting services would be announced through this type of website.

Reading the Business Newspapers

Government agencies are required to publicly advertise the RFPs and RFQs that they issue. There is usually at least one business newspaper in every region that is known as a "publication of record" for public announcements of this type. In the Seattle area where I am located, this newspaper is called the "Daily Journal of Commerce". Consultants who want to learn about opportunities can subscribe to either the printed or online version of these newspapers and scan them regularly for business opportunities.

Subscribing to a Bid Tracking Service

There are online services specifically designed to track business opportunities on a local, state, regional or national level. Consultants can subscribe to these services and specify the categories of opportunities that they are looking for. On a daily or weekly basis, the service will send an email digest of all opportunities in the geographical areas that the consultant has specified. These services are somewhat expensive but take most of the work out of searching for opportunities. These services are ideal for consultants who are seeking opportunities over a wide geographical area.

Working with Influencers

Many of your influencers in the security or construction industries may be registered on government agency websites or subscribe to business newspapers or bid tracking services. Often these influencers will hear about an opportunity for security consulting services and will tell you about it. I regularly get emails from influencers telling me about security consulting RFPs. In many cases, I have already heard about the RFP from another source, but I appreciate them thinking about me, nonetheless. Occasionally, an influencer will send me news concerning an RFP that I have not heard about, and I very much appreciate this.

Responding to RFPs and RFQs

Consultants should respond to RFPs and RFQs using the methods outlined in Chapter 9. For the most part, responding to RFPs issued by government agencies is very similar to responding to RFPs issued by private companies, with a few exceptions. Here are some of the special things that you may encounter when responding to an RFP for a government agency:

<u>Price Justification</u>

Most government agencies want to see a detailed breakdown of your pricing within your proposal. You usually must break down each project into a series of tasks and provide an estimate of the hours that each task will take.

Many agencies will not allow you to arbitrarily set your hourly rate – you must justify it using a formula that specifies your cost of labor, overhead, and profit. A most cases, a limit is set on the percentage of overhead and profit that the consultant can charge. The formula rarely produces a rounded number, and you are expected to charge the exact amount, not a penny more or less. On one government project that I did in the past, my billing rate was $101.52 per hour.

Because these formulas often result in an hourly rate well below what consultants normally charge, many consultants working on government projects choose to "pad" their estimates of how long it takes to complete each task to make up the difference. Although this seems to be a widely accepted practice in government contracting, I personally feel that this type of misrepresentation is unethical.

When using a subcontractor, you must indicate in your proposal the actual fee being paid to the subcontractor, plus the markup that you are adding to this amount. Like with overhead and profit, there is often a specified limit on the percentage of markup on subcontractors that can be charged.

Expense Limits

Most government agencies place strict limits on the types of expenses that they will reimburse and the maximum amounts that can be spent on certain items. The limits placed on travel expenses can be particularly restrictive, often requiring that the consultant pay certain expenses out of their own pocket if they want to travel comfortably.

MBE/WBE/SBE Requirements

Many government agencies encourage the participation of Minority Business Enterprise (MBE), Women Business Enterprise (WBE) and Small Business Enterprise (SBE) firms in all contracts that they award.

In some cases, a certain percentage of MBE/WBE/SBE participation is required. For example, on a $100,000 contract, the agency may require that at least 15% of the contract, or $15,000, be awarded to MBE/WBE/SBE firms. In order for a proposal to be considered responsive, it must show how it intends to meet this requirement.

In other cases, the use of MBE/WBE/SBE firms is voluntary but is rewarded during the proposal evaluation phase. For example, the agency may set a target goal for MBE/WBE/SBE participation at 20% of the contract value. Proposers who meet the 20% participation goal are awarded 30 additional points. Proposers who achieve only 10% participation would receive 15 additional points, and proposers who had 0% participation would receive no additional points.

Security consultants who are themselves MBE/WBE/SBE firms could obviously meet MBE/WBE/SBE requirements provided that they were properly registered as such. Registration typically takes place at the state level, but some local government agencies have registration processes as well. Consultants who qualify to register are urged to do so as early as possible so that everything is in place when they prepare their proposals.

Security consultants who are not MBE/WBE/SBE firms will need to hire an MBE/WBE/SBE subcontractor in order to meet mandatory participation requirements, or to be awarded additional points for voluntary participation.

It should be noted here that many of the larger security consulting firms and architectural and engineering firms are always on the lookout for qualified MBE/WBE/SBE firms to allow them to meet their participation requirements. Smaller security consulting firms who are MBE/WBE/SBE can often do a substantial amount of work just helping larger firms meet these requirements.

The status of MBE/WBE/SBE programs can shift with the political winds. Some states that once required MBE/WBE/SBE participation now ban the use of these types of programs entirely.

Pass-Through Requirements

Many state and local government agencies finance projects using money that they receive from federal government grants. In most cases, along with this money comes the stipulation that all contractors working on the project meet federal requirements in addition to any requirements that the agency itself imposes. This can have an effect on fees, expenses, wages, reporting requirements, and many other things.

When submitting a proposal on a project that is federally funded, make sure that you fully understand what, if any, federal requirements may apply. Often, a reference to a law will be made in the RFP ("*Contractor shall comply with Section 503 of the US Department of Labor Rehabilitation Act*"), but no specific details are provided. It is up to you to research the law to see what impact it may have on your work.

Consultant Rosters

To avoid the trouble and expense of using the RFP process when hiring a consultant for smaller jobs, some agencies maintain what is known as a "consultant roster". The consultant roster is a list of consultants in various disciplines that have been prequalified by the agency. The consultant roster typically includes architects, engineers, land surveyors, and other design professionals, but may also include security consultants.

To get on the consultant roster, the consultant applies by submitting a qualifications statement. In some cases, this can be done at any time, but in other cases, an opportunity to get on the roster occurs only once per year.

Once on the roster, the consultant may be called by the agency and given projects up to a certain dollar amount, often $15,000 or $20,000. Projects over this amount still need to go through the RFP process. If there is more than one consultant in a category on the roster, projects would be assigned on a rotational basis between consultants. There is never a guarantee of any specific amount of work, and some consultants may not receive any work at all as a result of being on the roster.

Consultant rosters last for a specified time period, typically one to three years. Once a roster has expired, consultants must reapply to get on the next one.

When hiring a security consultant, some government agencies will use the consultant roster system to get around the requirement to issue an RFP. When they find a consultant that they want to work with, they suggest that the consultant apply to get on the roster. A short time later, they use the roster to hire the consultant. This can work well because the cost of most security consulting projects usually falls below the roster limit, and because very few if any other security consultants are likely to be on the roster.

Indefinite Delivery, Indefinite Quantity Contracts

Many government agencies use what are known as Indefinite Delivery, Indefinite Quantity (IDIQ) contracts. These contracts are used when the agency knows it will need certain goods or services over time but cannot specify exact quantities or delivery dates.

The period of performance of the contract is for a fixed period (such as 3 years), with options for renewal at the sole discretion of the agency for a period not to exceed a specified period (such as 5 years). Each IDIQ contract has a maximum value that cannot be exceeded.

IDIQ contracts are somewhat similar to consultant rosters, but unlike rosters, an IDIQ is an actual contract with terms, conditions, and pricing established upfront, and the consultant is usually given a guarantee of a certain minimum amount of work. Once a consultant is awarded an IDIQ contract, task orders for specific projects may be issued by the agency as needed until the maximum value of the contract is reached.

To be awarded an IDIQ contract, consultants must usually compete for the work by responding to an RFQ using the methods outlined in Chapter 9.

Can I Sell Proactively to Government Agencies?

Most of the discussions above assume that a government agency has already identified the need for a security consultant and has decided to hire one using the RFP process or one of the other procurement methods described above. What about government agencies who don't know what services that independent security consultants provide, or haven't yet been convinced to hire one?

Security consultants can make sales calls to government agencies just like they do to any other type of prospective client. In many cases, an agency needs to be educated on the benefits of using an independent security consultant or needs help in finding a specific consultant that can meet their needs.

Consultants are encouraged to respond to marketing inquiries that they receive from government agencies, and proactively call upon agencies within their marketing area that may need their services. However, before investing too much time in working with an agency, consultants need to remember that the procurement laws that agencies must follow are always lingering in the background.

It is not uncommon for an agency to call a consultant and ask for help with a security consulting project. The consultant eagerly responds, assuming that they have an excellent chance of being hired. The consultant spends a lot of time meeting with the client and touring the facilities, and then prepares a proposal that includes a detailed scope of work.

A few weeks later, the consultant hears back from the agency saying that the cost of the project is beyond their discretionary purchasing authority, and that they must issue a formal RFP. When the consultant receives the RFP, they see that much of the scope of work within the document has been directly copied from the proposal that they previously submitted. They attend the preproposal conference and see that there are at least fifteen other firms in attendance. At the conclusion of the RFP process, the project is awarded to another firm. The original consultant is heartbroken and angry that they spent so much time working with the agency and have nothing to show for it.

The bottom line is this: fully understand a government agency's procurement policies before you start working with them. When providing information and assistance to an agency prior to the issuance of an RFP, understand that this is no guarantee that you will receive work from them, or receive preferential treatment during any upcoming RFP process.

Chapter 11 - Selling to Architects and Engineers

Architects and engineers (A/Es) are a major source of consulting work for independent security consultants. This is especially true for technical security consultants, who may perform a majority of their work for A/Es. Certain types of security management consultants may also be called in by A/Es when their specialized expertise is needed in planning security for a new facility.

Selling to A/Es is different from selling to other types of clients, and security consultants who wish to be successful in this market need to understand these differences.

The Need for Architects and Engineers

Architects and engineers provide design services for new construction projects and major renovation projects. Almost every client who is building a new facility or remodeling an existing one will hire an A/E to design the project. While some clients have in-house resources that can be used to design smaller projects, most lack the capability to design larger projects. The law also requires that projects above a certain size be designed by A/Es that are licensed in the state where the project will be constructed.

Once designed, the project will typically be put out to bid, and one or more contractors will be asked to submit bids on the project. The client will then select a contractor and construction begins. In most cases, the A/E who did the design will stay on to oversee the project and serve as the client's representative during the construction process.

Design Team

Because of the complexity of building construction, a team of various types of professionals is needed to complete the building design. This team is known as the "design team". The design team typically includes architects, interior designers, specification writers, electrical engineers, mechanical engineers, civil engineers, landscape architects, and many more. In some rare cases, all of these professionals may be employed by a single firm, but much more commonly, the design team will be made up of multiple firms.

The design team is typically led by an architectural firm, who has the prime contract with the owner. All members of the design team who are not direct employees of the architectural firm work as subcontractors to the architectural firm. For example, the client may hire XYZ Architects to design a building. All architectural and interior design work would be done in-house by XYZ employees, but mechanical and electrical engineering work would be subcontracted to an outside firm, ABC Engineering. All other specialized design work would be similarly subcontracted to other experts in specialized fields.

There are sometimes exceptions to the process described above. When designing certain types of industrial facilities, such as a manufacturing plant, the majority of the work is engineering work rather than architectural work. In these cases, the client will usually hire an engineering firm rather than an architectural firm to lead the design team. In these cases, an architectural firm could be hired as a subcontractor to the engineering firm rather than the other way around.

When a project requires security consulting services, a security consultant would be asked to join the design team. In many cases, the security consultant would contract directly with the A/E firm leading the design team. Occasionally, the security consultant may be asked to work for one of the other subcontractors, such as the project electrical engineer.

Design Process Used by Architects and Engineers

The architectural and engineering design process used in the United States today is more than 150 years old. This process has its own language, culture, and traditions. People from outside of the design and construction industry often feel like they have landed on another planet when sitting in on a design meeting for the first time.

Security consultants who wish to work with A/Es need to have a basic understanding of the traditional A/E design process, and learn the language used by these design professionals. For the most part, security consultants will need to adapt their processes to meet the needs of the A/E – not the other way around. Security consultants who try to work outside of the traditional A/E process will likely face stiff resistance and ultimately fail when working on design projects led by A/Es.

Architectural Design Phases

A structured process is used by A/Es to design buildings and other facilities. This process takes the project from an initial idea all the way to a completed structure that is ready to be occupied. The traditional A/E process typically consists of at least the following six phases:

Pre-Design Phase

The predesign phase includes the development of an architectural program which fully defines project requirements in narrative form. The architectural program identifies the functions that will be required in the building, the approximate space required for each function, and the relative locations of each function within the building. The architectural program is very important because it becomes the basis for all design activities that follow.

Schematic Design (SD) Phase

The schematic design phase is when the concepts identified within the architectural program start to become transformed into an actual design. During schematic design, study drawings that illustrate the concepts of the design are presented to the client for review. Often, multiple alternatives are presented and the best ideas from each are combined into a single design. During this phase, zoning and building code requirements are also researched. At the conclusion of this phase, the client and architect agree on a schematic design, and this becomes the basis for the project moving forward. Rough project costs can also be estimated at this point.

Design Development (DD) Phase

The design development phase takes the schematic design to the next level. Much more detailed information is provided on exactly how the building will be constructed and what types of materials will be used. Specific details on the structural, mechanical and electrical systems that will be used in the building are provided.

At the conclusion of this phase, the client carefully reviews the design to be sure that it meets expectations. Making major changes to the design beyond this point can be difficult so it is important that the client be happy with the design before proceeding further. Detailed project costs can be much more accurately estimated at the conclusion of this phase.

Construction Documents (CD) Phase

The construction documents phase of the project creates the final documents that will be needed by the contractor to build the building. The construction documents are what the contractor uses to bid on the project, so they need to show everything that has an impact on the cost of materials and labor. Once the contractor's bid is accepted, the construction documents are signed by all parties and become an attachment to the construction contract. For this reason, these documents are sometimes also called "contract documents".

Because they are so important, construction documents typically provide much more detail than the documents produced during the design development phase. Construction documents also include detailed written specifications on the materials to be used and the processes to be followed during the construction phase.

Bidding and Negotiations Phase

During the bidding and negotiations phase, the construction documents are issued to contractors to obtain bids. While this process is typically managed by the client, the A/E helps the client during this phase by answering bidder questions, issuing addenda, evaluating bids, and helping to negotiate the final contract with the selected bidder.

Construction Phase Services

During the construction phase, the A/E is typically hired to watch over the project and provide a variety of construction administration services. These services can include attending weekly construction meetings, responding to requests-for-information (RFIs) from contractors, reviewing and approving change orders, processing contractor payment requests, conducting a final inspection of the project, and preparing a punch-list of items requiring correction.

Security consultants working with A/Es on design projects may be asked to provide services during some or all of the six phases outlined above. While it is beneficial to include a security consultant as early as the predesign phase, many A/Es don't even begin to think about security until the DD or CD phases. At this point, it can be difficult or impossible to correct problems in the design that may have a negative impact on security.

Alternative Project Delivery Approaches

The architectural design process described above is sometimes known as the "design-bid-build" process. This process has been used for over a hundred years and is still the most commonly used process on larger new construction projects. However, in recent years, some clients have become frustrated with the time and expense required by this traditional process and have sought out other alternatives. The two most common of these alternatives are the "design/build" process, and the general contractor/construction manager (GC/CM) process.

When using the design/build process, the client hires a single entity, usually a general contractor, to both design and build the building. The advantage of this approach is that the client can hold a single party responsible for the project, avoiding the finger-pointing that can often occur between the A/E and the contractor. This approach can also reduce project completion time, as the contractor can begin construction on some parts of the project before the design work is fully complete.

When using the GC/CM approach, the contractor is selected early in the design process, usually on the basis of qualifications and not price. The contractor then acts as a consultant during the design process, offering advice on how the building can be built better or at less cost. At about late DD stage, the contractor and client agree on a guaranteed maximum price, known as the maximum allowable construction cost (MACC). Clients who prefer the GC/CM approach say that it offers many advantages, including better control of costs, more practical building designs, fewer change orders, and shorter project completion times.

The use of an alternative project approach can have an impact on the work performed by the security consultant. For example, it has been my experience that design/build contractors are notoriously cheap when it comes to security and will use the absolutely least expensive types of security systems unless directed otherwise by the client.

When working on GC/CM projects, I have found that it is extremely important to get all security requirements completely defined by the early DD phase. This is when the contractor estimates the MACC, and any security systems not included in the design at this point will likely be omitted from the project.

How Clients Choose A/E Firms for Projects

Most clients use a competitive procurement process to hire the A/E firm that they will design their new construction and renovation project. This competitive process is required by law for most government agency clients, and is also commonly used by many private companies when choosing an A/E.

The Request for Qualifications (RFQ) process described in Chapter 9 is the most commonly used method of procuring A/E services. A/Es wishing to be considered for a project submit a Statement of Qualifications (SOQ). The SOQ is evaluated by the client and a shortlist of firms is selected to be interviewed. After the interviews, the client selects the A/E firm that it wishes to use for its project.

Assembling a Design Team

Because a large team of professionals are required to design most projects, the SOQ submitted by the A/E firm must usually include qualifications on the entire design team, not just the A/E firm itself.

To create the SOQ, the A/E firm must first assemble its design team. This involves the selection of structural engineers, mechanical engineers, electrical engineers, civil engineers and consultants of all other types, including security consultants.

How does the A/E go about choosing the firms it wishes to have on its project team? In many cases, the A/E will have established relationships with one or two firms in each category and will use these same firms on a majority of its projects. In other cases, the A/E will select team members that have specific expertise in the type of facility that the RFQ is requesting services for. For example, when responding to an RFQ for a courthouse project, the A/E would probably choose to use team members who had previous experience with courthouses.

It is important to understand that when the client is evaluating the A/E's SOQ, they are evaluating the design team as a whole, not just the A/E firm itself. Most A/Es recognize this, so attempt to fill their team with only the best qualified professionals in every area. Sometimes projects are won or lost based on the qualifications of the consultants being used, so A/Es select their team members very carefully.

When an A/E firm is short-listed by the client and selected to be interviewed, the A/E will often be asked to bring key team members to the interview session. When the A/E is awarded the project, it is expected that the A/E will use the team members included in the SOQ to perform the actual work on the project.

Getting On A/E Project Teams

Many RFQs issued by clients will include specific requirements to include a security consultant on the design team. This requirement is commonly found on government projects such as courthouses, police stations, and other public facilities. For these types of projects, the A/E will usually be actively seeking the services of a qualified security consultant.

For other types of projects, the RFQ may not specifically ask for the services of a security consultant, but the A/E may decide to include one on the project team anyway. Many clients have security concerns, and by including a security consultant on the design team, the A/E can demonstrate that the firm takes a proactive approach on the issue of security. This can distinguish one A/E firm from another during the evaluation process, and can be a positive selling point for the A/E.

How do security consultants get asked to join design teams? There are two methods for doing this.

Method #1 is to proactively market your services to A/E firms within your market area using the techniques explained in Chapter 8. If this marketing is done effectively, A/Es will remember who you are and will seek you out when they receive an RFQ that includes a requirement for security consulting. Security consultants who specialize in specific types of projects should make it their mission to contact every A/E firm who is known to design projects in their area of specialization. For instance, if you are a hospital security consultant, you should make yourself known to every A/E in your chosen geographical region that has a reputation for designing hospitals.

Method #2 is to specifically reach out to A/Es when you become aware that an RFQ for A/E services in your specialty area is being issued. For example, if you are a courthouse security consultant, you should always be on the lookout for RFQs for A/E services involving courthouse projects. When you spot this type of RFQ, you should reach out to the A/E firms in your marketing database to see if they are already aware of the opportunity and ask if the firm intends to submit a SOQ. If so, ask if you can join the team as their security consultant.

To increase your chances of success, you should market using both methods: 1) proactively reach out to A/E firms in advance of project opportunities to establish a relationship; and 2) contact A/E firms immediately once specific RFQ opportunities become known.

It is customary for consultants in specialty areas such as security to be asked to join more than one A/E team during the RFQ process. For example, on one RFQ for a government office building I responded to in the past, I was on four separate A/E teams, two of which were short-listed.

Consultants who choose to join multiple teams need to operate in a highly ethical manner and go out of their way to treat all teams equally. Information about one team should never be shared with another team.

Some A/Es will require that consultants give them an "exclusive", meaning that if they are given the opportunity to join the A/E's team, they must agree not to join any other teams. Consultants should think carefully before agreeing to exclusive arrangements, as they can greatly reduce the consultant's odds of winning a project. I usually only agree to exclusives with A/E firms that I have worked with on previous projects and whom I know stand a good chance of winning the project.

Your Ally: The A/E's Marketing Department

Most A/E firms will have a department that specializes in selling the A/E firm's services and in responding to RFQs and other opportunities. This department is usually called the "Marketing Department" or "Business Development Department". In smaller firms, this department may consist of only one person, in larger firms, this department could have a dozen or more employees.

Security consultants should get to know the key people in the marketing departments at the major A/E firms in their practice area. These people usually do a good job of staying on top of potential opportunities and are always looking for ways to strengthen their project teams through the use of specialty consultants.

Marketing departments act as a support department to the principals of the A/E firm and usually don't select consultants on their own but can be highly influential in the making of this decision.

You should stay in frequent contact with these marketing people to remind them of your service offerings. Also, when you hear about a RFQ or other opportunity in the A/E's practice area, give them a quick call to ask them if they are aware of it. Even if they already know about it, they are usually appreciative that you took the time to call.

When an A/E's marketing department asks you to provide your qualifications, project history, and other information, respond quickly. Most A/E marketing departments operate under tight deadlines and often have to assemble large SOQs in just a matter of days. Providing information quickly and reliably can help set you apart from other consultants and help you to get invited to join more project teams.

Standard Form 330

When joining an A/E team going after a government project, you will more than likely be asked to submit a Standard Form 330 (SF330) Architect-Engineer Qualifications. This is a federal government form but is also used by a wide variety of state and local government agencies and even some private clients.

The SF330 asks for the qualifications and experience of all members of the A/E team, as well as a history of projects completed by the A/E firm and individual team members. The practice area of team members and the types of projects are classified using codes given on the form.

On projects where security is of importance, the security consultant's qualifications and experience must typically be included on the SF330.

The SF330 can be downloaded for free from the US Government General Services Administration (GSA). Security consultants who intend to join A/E project teams should download this form in advance and fill out the resume and other appropriate sections. In most cases, the A/E will submit one master SF330 for the entire team, but having the information in the correct format from all team members in advance greatly speeds up the preparation process.

Lunch and Learns

One common way that supplier's market to A/E firms is through the use of "lunch and learn" programs. The sponsor of the lunch and learn program conducts a one-hour educational seminar on a topic of interest to A/Es and agrees to provide a free lunch for all participants. In most cases, the lunch and learn sessions are conducted at lunchtime at the A/E firm's office.

To be acceptable to A/E firms, the lunch and learn session should be educational in nature and not just a sales pitch. Sessions that discuss new design techniques or address issues that have recently been in the news are usually very well-received.

I have found lunch and learns to be a particularly effective way for security consultants to market their services to A/Es. Many architects and engineers find the subject of security to be fascinating and are eager to learn more about it.

Conducting a lunch and learn can be somewhat expensive because of the need to provide a catered lunch for the participants. However, I have personally had great success with lunch and learns. I have almost always received a project as a result of the sessions I have conducted, making the investment worthwhile. Your results may vary.

Larger A/E firms will have a person on staff whose job includes coordinating lunch and learn sessions with suppliers. If you intend to include lunch and learns as a part of your marketing strategy, get to know who this person is at the major A/E firms in your practice area. There can be a several month waiting list to get on the calendar at larger A/E firms.

Considerations When Working with A/Es

Here are some additional things to consider when working with A/E firms:

- When working for an A/E, all consultants will normally be required to sign an industry-standard consultant agreement. Most architects use standard agreements provided by the American Institute of Architects (AIA), such as *AIA Form C401 Standard Form of Agreement between Architect and Consultant.* The agreement with the A/E will normally require that the consultants accept all terms and conditions that were stated in the A/Es agreement with the owner. Be sure that you fully understand all contract requirements before signing an agreement.

- When working for an A/E on a project for a government agency, all of the special requirements stated in Chapter 10 will normally apply. This will have an impact on the rates that you can charge, how you will be reimbursed for expenses, and which, if any, MBE/WBE/SBE participation requirements you must comply with.

- When working with A/Es, the "pay when paid" rule will normally apply. This means that you won't get paid until the A/E gets paid. It is common to wait 60 or 90 days to get paid when working with A/Es. Discuss payment terms before you sign an agreement with the A/E and make sure you have the ability to survive while you are waiting to get paid.
- When working for an A/E, there is a strict chain of command that must be followed. All communications between you and other parties must normally pass through the A/E. Communicating directly with the owner, contractor, or other consultants is a no-no unless specific permission has been given by the A/E.
- When working with an A/E, written documentation of all communications is essential. Follow-up all telephone calls with a confirming email or memo. Keep written notes of all meetings and verbal instructions given by the A/E. Review meeting notes prepared by others and quickly correct any misunderstandings in writing.
- Situations may arise when there is disagreement between you and the A/E concerning what is best for the project. For example, the architect may propose using a certain type of lock hardware that looks good but provides very little security. Or the architect may want you to place a camera in a location that is inconspicuous but doesn't provide good coverage of the intended viewing area. Whenever possible, conflicts of this type should be resolved privately between you and the A/E and not in the presence of the owner. You should support any final decision made by the A/E, even if you do not agree with it, but be sure to document your concerns in writing.

Chapter 12 - Creating a Business Plan

A business plan is a written document that describes your proposed security consulting business: what you plan to do and how you plan to do it. Just like every pilot should prepare a flight plan before beginning a flight, every business owner should prepare a business plan before starting a business.

Purpose of Business Plan

The purpose of a business plan is to provide a roadmap for operating your business. The business plan should summarize the services that your security consulting firm will provide and how you intend to sell these services to clients. The business plan should also include financial projections that indicate how much money will be required to start your consulting practice, and monthly cash flow projections for at least the first twenty-four months of operation.

Business plans serve two purposes: 1) they provide a framework for the business owner to operate the business; and 2) they provide information to help obtain financing for the business from banks or outside investors.

Business owners seeking an investment from outsiders will need to prepare a more elaborate, formal business plan in order to sell their business concept to a bank or investors. Business owners financing their business themselves can get by with a less formal business plan because it will be used only as an internal tool to help them manage their business.

There are numerous resources on the internet that provide detailed guidelines on how to create a formal business plan. One good source of information is the Small Business Administration (SBA). Most formal business plans include information on at least the following topics:

- Description of company.
- How the company will be organized and managed.
- Services that the company will provide.

- The market for the services being provided.
- Competitive advantages and disadvantages.
- Marketing and sales strategies.
- Financial projections.
- How the company will be financed.

Financial Projections for the First 24 Months

The first twenty-four months will be the most crucial in determining the success or failure of your new consulting practice. It is essential that your business plan includes financial projections for this critical period. These projections will tell you how much money that you will need to launch your practice, and how much money that you will need to operate the business until such a time as it begins to generate enough cash to sustain itself.

To create financial projections requires the following steps:

Step #1 – Determine Start-Up Costs

Start-up costs are the amount of money that it will take to get your security consulting practice started. This requires totaling up the costs of all tools, equipment and materials that will be required to open up your business. Initial costs for professional fees, licenses, and insurance should also be included in this total.

Start-up costs can vary greatly from person to person. Many people starting their practice may already own much of the equipment that they need, allowing them to reduce their start-up costs. Those who have the ability to develop their own website can eliminate the substantial cost of having this done professionally.

The table below provides an example of what the start-up costs might be for a one-person security consulting firm that will be operated out of a home.

Computer and office equipment	$3,000
Printing costs for stationery and brochures	$500
Website development and set-up costs	$7,000
Professional fees (accountant and attorney)	$1,000
Business licenses and registration fees	$500
Business insurance	$3,500
Telephone and internet service set-up costs	$500
Business software	$1,000
Consultant tools (camera, recorder, light meter)	$700
Online subscriptions to business publications	$300
Office supplies	$500
Miscellaneous	$1,500
Total Start-Up Costs	**$20,000**

Total Start-Up Costs

Step #2 – Determine Monthly Overhead Costs

Monthly overhead costs are the amount of money that must be spent each month to operate the consulting business. The table below provides an example of what the monthly overhead costs might be for a one-person security consulting firm that will be operated out of a home.

Like with start-up costs, monthly overhead costs can vary greatly from consultant to consultant depending on the consultant's specific circumstances and area of practice. Because there will always be costs that you cannot anticipate, it is usually better to guess higher rather than lower when estimating costs.

The table below provides an example of what the monthly overhead costs might be for a one-person security consulting firm that will be operated out of a home.

Advertising & Marketing	$500
Computer & Internet	$200
Continuing Education	$200
Professional Fees	$200
Insurance	$400
Office Supplies	$100
Publications	$100
Software	$100
Taxes	$400
Telephone	$100
Tools & Equipment	$200
Miscellaneous	$1,000
Total Monthly Overhead Costs	**$3,500**

Total Monthly Overhead Costs

Step #3 – Establish Personal Living Allowance

A personal living allowance is the minimum amount of money that you would need to support you and your family during the first twenty-four months of business operation, including the costs of health insurance.

This amount can vary greatly from person to person. The beginning consultant that is already receiving a retirement pension from a previous employer, or who has a spouse with a well-paying job and good benefits, may require no living allowance at all. A person who is the sole provider for a young family may require a substantial living allowance in order for their family to survive.

Please understand that your living allowance is not a tax-deductible business expense but is included in your financial projections because it affects the total amount of money that you must have on hand in order to start your practice.

Step #4 – Create Cash Flow Projections

Cash flow projections show how much money will be going out and coming in on a monthly basis.

Calculating the amount of cash going out is relatively straightforward – you simply add your monthly overhead costs to your monthly living allowance to determine the amount of cash going out. Determining the amount of cash coming in is much more challenging. Unlike estimating costs, which are generally predictable, estimating income is far trickier. To estimate monthly income, it is necessary to answer the following questions:

- How quickly will you be able to attract clients?
- What types of services you will be able to sell?
- What will clients pay for these services?
- How quickly will you get paid after services are provided?

I wish I could tell you that I had a magic formula for answering these questions, but I don't. The answers can vary greatly depending on the types of services being offered, the consultant's marketing and sales abilities, and present economic conditions.

Based on what I have observed when helping other new consultants get started, I have found that it can take from six to eighteen months for an independent security consulting practice to reach the point where monthly income is equal to or greater than monthly expenses. This is often called the "break-even" point.

In some rare cases, the new consultant may already have one or two projects in hand when they start their consulting practice. This type of situation allows the consultant to start generating cash within the first couple of months of operation and is ideal.

A much more common scenario is for the new consultant to have to wait several months for the first project to come in, and then wait a month or two more before the first payment is finally received.

The tables below provide an illustration of a two-year cash flow projection for a new security management consulting practice. The monthly income figures are an estimate of what a new consultant might be able to bring in during the first twenty-four months of business operation.

Observe that both income and expenses can vary from month to month. If sales and marketing efforts are going well, you can expect income to increase over time, but income in the security consulting business is rarely consistent and may go up and down from month to month. In most cases, as income begins to increase, expenses also increase somewhat, so the monthly expense amounts in this projections have been adjusted upward in the later months to reflect this.

Month	Monthly Income	Monthly Overhead	Living Allowance	Cash Flow
1	$0	$3,500	$4,000	-$7,500
2	$0	$3,500	$4,000	-$7,500
3	$0	$3,500	$4,000	-$7,500
4	$6,000	$3,500	$4,000	-$1,500
5	$7,500	$3,500	$4,000	$0
6	$9,000	$3,500	$4,000	$1,500
7	$12,000	$3,500	$4,000	$4,500
8	$9,000	$3,500	$4,000	$1,500
9	$7,500	$3,500	$4,000	$0
10	$13,500	$3,500	$4,000	$6,000
11	$15,000	$3,500	$4,000	$7,500
12	$16,500	$3,500	$4,000	$9,000

Year #1 Cash Flow Projections

Month	Monthly Income	Monthly Overhead	Living Allowance	Cash Flow
13	$12,000	$3,500	$4,000	$4,500
14	$18,000	$3,500	$4,000	$10,500
15	$8,000	$4,000	$4,000	$0
16	$10,500	$4,000	$4,000	$2,500
17	$13,500	$4,000	$4,000	$5,500
18	$16,500	$4,000	$4,000	$8,500
19	$13,500	$4,000	$4,000	$5,500
20	$19,500	$4,000	$4,000	$11,500
21	$21,000	$4,000	$4,000	$13,000
22	$13,500	$4,500	$4,000	$5,000
23	$13,500	$4,500	$4,000	$5,000
24	$15,000	$4,500	$4,000	$6,500

Year #2 Cash Flow Projections

Please note that, in the cash flow projections above, there is a negative cash flow for the first four months that the business is in operation. This means that the business is paying out more in expenses than it is receiving in income. In order for the business to survive, an amount of money must be on-hand to pay these expenses. I call this the amount the "operating deficit", and in the example above, it equals $24,000 for the first four months. In the example above, it is not until the fifth month that the business breaks even. In Month 6, the business begins to generate positive cash flow.

Determining the Amount of Cash Needed to Get Started

To determine the amount of cash required to get started, you add the Total Start-Up Costs to the. Using the examples above, the minimum amount of money needed to start your security consulting practice would be $44,000 ($20,000 Start-Up Costs plus $24,000 Operating Deficit).

Most beginning consultants tend to greatly underestimate startup costs and monthly overhead costs, and greatly overestimate the amount of monthly income that they will receive during the first year. This mistake is the primary reason why many new security consultants run out of money and are forced to close their business and look for full-time employment.

It is recommended that you take a conservative approach when estimating income and expenses and error on the side of pessimism rather than optimism when making your cash flow projections. It is far better to enjoy the benefits of reaching the break-even point early than it is to run out of money just when your consulting business is about to become a success.

Prospective security consultants who don't have enough money to get started have two choices: they can borrow the additional money that they need or can wait to start their practice until they have saved up the needed amount.

I would personally never consider starting a consulting practice using borrowed money. I feel that having to make a monthly loan payment or satisfy the needs of an investor would put additional pressure on me that I wouldn't want when attempting to launch a business. Your personal circumstances or philosophy may cause you to make a different decision.

If you are presently working at a job, it is often better to wait a little longer to save up additional money than it is to quit now and start your practice without adequate funds. Exercising a little patience in delaying the start of your practice can increase your chances of success in the long run.

Chapter 13 – Making the Leap

You have read through the previous chapters of this book, and you have decided to make the leap – you are ready to launch your own consulting practice. Here are some suggested steps to help you to get started.

Is Now the Right Time?

1. Review your financial situation to determine if this is the right time to start a new consulting practice. Do you have the money it will take to start your business as discussed in Chapter 12? Do you have enough income and/or savings to sustain yourself and your family through the time it will take to get your practice established?
2. Determine what your options for health insurance will be once you are self-employed, including what types of coverage will be available and what they will cost. If you or any family member has special medical needs, the availability of affordable health insurance could be a major factor in deciding whether or not to go out on your own.
3. Do you have, or are you on the path to acquiring the four areas of expertise needed to operate a successful security consulting practice as outlined in Chapter 3?

Talk With Your Family

Discuss your proposed plans with your spouse or partner and other family members. Talk about how things might change when you become a self-employed independent security consultant: the need to work long hours, the possible need to have a home office, and the unpredictable nature of your income.

Explain the types of support that you will need from family members and be sure that they are on board with your plans to start a new security consulting practice.

Before You Quit Your Present Job

Here are some things that you should consider doing before you leave your present job:

1. It is often easier to obtain credit when you have a full-time job than it is when you are self-employed. If you need to buy a car on credit, refinance your house, or obtain an additional credit card, now might be the time to do it.
2. Take advantage of any health, dental, and vision benefits that your employer currently offers. Depending on your specific situation, the insurance coverage that you are able to obtain as a self-employed person may not be as generous as that currently offered by your employer. If you need new glasses or a dental crown, now might be the time to get them.
3. Create a directory of your industry contacts to make sure that you have the current telephone number and email address of everyone in the industry that you currently know or work with. The information in this directory should be included in your marketing database when you start your consulting practice.
4. Create a list of major projects within your organization that you have completed in the past three to five years. This could include things like rewriting your organization's security policies manual, developing a new training program, or designing a security system for a new facility that your company constructed. This information should be included in your consultant's resume when you start your practice.
5. Review the list of things necessary to plan and start your consulting practice that have been previously listed in this book. Try to do as many things as possible well in advance of the date that you intend to start your practice. The more that you do in advance, the easier it will be to hit the ground running when you officially get started.

Launching Your Practice

- Establish an official start date to launch your consulting practice. If you are presently employed, give your employer ample notice of your pending departure. Keep in mind that former employers are often a direct or indirect source of future consulting work, so try not to burn any bridges.
- Find another independent security consultant to act as your mentor. Stay in close contact with your mentor as you start the operation of your security consulting business. Tell your mentor your goals for the first twelve months of your business and ask your mentor to hold you accountable for achieving these goals.
- Once you have given notice to your employer, begin to notify all of your industry contacts of the change that you are about to make. Don't forget to notify suppliers and professionals in related fields who you have worked with in the past. Tell any contacts that you feel might be prospective clients about your plans and let them know that you will be calling on them in the near future.
- Issue press releases announcing the start of your new consulting practice to all appropriate publications. These publications should include local business newspapers, organizational newsletters, and magazines that are specific to your area of practice. There are numerous resources on the internet that provide step-by-step instructions for issuing an effective press release.
- Immediately begin conducting the sales and marketing activities as outlined in Chapter 8. Remember that your initial job as an independent security consultant is to sell your services, and for the immediate future, you should be spending a large portion of each day selling. Recognize that selling is not easy but must be done in order to succeed as a consultant.

Can I Start Consulting on a Part Time Basis While I'm Employed?

Many prospective security consultants ask the question: "Can I start my security consulting practice part-time while I am still working at my present job?" The answer depends entirely on the types of consulting services that you intend to provide, the types of clients that you plan to serve, and your present employment situation.

Certain types of consultants, such as forensic security consultants, can often work effectively on a part-time basis, while other types of consultants, such as technical security consultants, may find it difficult to meet their client's needs unless they are available full-time.

When contemplating starting a consulting practice on a part-time basis, the following should be considered:

- Most clients expect that their security consultant will be available during normal business hours. Having to wait days to get a telephone call returned or weeks to schedule a meeting is not acceptable to most clients. Along the same lines, communicating with vendors of security products and services and other people associated with consulting projects must usually take place during a weekday, not at night or on the weekend.
- Even if only working part-time, consultants should be properly licensed and insured and have all tools and equipment necessary to do a professional job. Often, the monthly overhead of a part-time consultant will be only slightly less than that of a full-time consultant, even though monthly income will be significantly less. This can make it difficult to earn a profit.
- Marketing a part-time security consulting practice can take almost as much effort as marketing a full-time security consulting practice. Many marketing activities, such as making telephone calls and going on sales appointments, must be done on a weekday.
- Working as a consultant on a part-time basis can be unfair to your present employer. Even if calls and emails related

to your consulting practice are made during lunch or on your breaks, having to deal with these issues during your workday can cause you to lose focus and become a less effective employee. Needing to take frequent days off to perform consulting projects can also be detrimental to the business needs of your employer.

Consulting on a part-time basis often works well when the part-time consultant is working as a subcontractor to another established security consultant.

For example, a security management consultant might hire a person that is presently working as a security director to write a policies and procedures manual. The prime consultant would handle all interactions with the client, while the security director works behind the scenes doing the writing. This work could easily be done at home at night or during the weekend and would not interfere with the security director's regular job.

Similarly, a forensic consultant retained by a lawyer might be able to do most work related to a case after hours at home and only have to take time off from work when needed for depositions or testimony in court.

Something I definitely don't recommend doing: Operating your part-time consulting business on your employer's time using your employer's equipment and supplies. Sadly, I know several people in security management positions at big companies who have been doing this for years.

Chapter 14 - Taking Your Practice to the Next Level

Many consultants, after having successfully established a security consulting practice, are happy to continue to work as sole practitioners and see no reason to make any type of change.

Other security consultants, having enjoyed a certain level of success, ask: "What's next? – how do I grow my security consulting practice and take it to the next level?"

Within this chapter, we will explore some methods that consultants commonly use to leverage their capabilities and grow their business.

Teaming

Security consultants often choose to expand their capabilities by forming "partnering" or "teaming" relationships with other independent consultants or consulting firms. Teaming arrangements can allow consultants to work on projects that they otherwise would stand no chance of winning on their own.

Teaming arrangements are often formed to go after specific projects but can also be ongoing arrangements between parties that go on for years. Reasons for forming teaming arrangements can include:

- A project requires a type of expertise that the individual consultant does not possess. For example, a security management consultant may encounter a project opportunity that requires both physical security expertise and cybersecurity expertise.
- A project requires that services be performed at multiple geographical locations, some of which are not cost effective for the individual consultant to serve. For example, a Miami-based consultant may not be able to competitively provide services to a project located in Alaska.
- The project is too large for the individual consultant to complete within the allocated time frame. For example, the client may want security assessments for 40 sites completed within 30 days, which would be impossible for a single consultant to perform.

- The project requires a certain type of license or certification that the individual consultant does not possess. For example, an RFP may require that someone on the consulting team possess a CISSP certification, and the individual consultant doesn't possess this credential.
- The chances of winning a project would be greatly improved by adding a well-known and highly respected team member in a specific practice area. For example, the chances of an individual consultant winning a project that included requirements for bomb blast analysis could be greatly improved by teaming with a highly recognized bomb blast expert.
- The chances of winning a project would be improved by partnering with a team member that the client already knows and trusts. For example, a technical security consultant going after a security design project for a large manufacturing plant might greatly benefit by teaming up with the engineering firm that already does the mechanical and electrical design work for the plant.

While teaming arrangements can offer many benefits, there can also be some risks. Here are some things to think about before entering into a teaming arrangement:

- Most clients will want to contract with a single company that is responsible for performing all aspects of the security consulting project. The most common arrangement is to have one firm act as the "prime consultant" and enter into contract with the client. All other team members then act as subcontractors to the prime consultant. Traditionally, the consultant who is performing the largest percentage of the work would act as prime, but exceptions are sometimes made because of previous relationships between the client and one of the firms, or to comply with licensing or insurance requirements.
- Know who you are teaming with. Use ample due diligence to verify the credentials of any team members who are unknown to you and who you may be working with for the very first time.

- A person who you have known for many years and maybe even consider to be a friend may perform differently than expected when you team up with them. If possible, work with people on a few smaller projects to gauge their actual performance before teaming up with them on a larger project.

- Many teaming arrangements are made verbally or through a handshake arrangement between the parties. Although this is commonly done, I highly recommend that a formal written agreement between all parties be drafted at the inception of the project. This agreement should spell out in detail the roles and responsibilities of each team member, the project schedule, the work product and deliverables to be produced by each party, and how each party shall be compensated and when.

- On some very large projects, it may be beneficial for teaming arrangements to be formalized through the creation of a separate legal entity, such as a corporation. Team members should consult with a legal advisor to determine the advantages and disadvantages of doing this.

- A single team member should be appointed to serve as the point of contact with the client. This team member would typically be the prime consultant. All communications to and from the client should be funneled through this team member.

- To the greatest extent possible, all reports and other work products delivered to the client should be consistent in appearance. All reports should use the same format, fonts, and terminology. It often works best to have a single party be assigned the responsibility of "master report writer". All other team members submit their work in rough form to the master report writer, who then combines the work of all team members into a single, unified report using a consistent format.

- Teaming arrangements work best when there is complete transparency, and the client is fully aware that the project is being performed by a group of independent consulting firms rather than just a single firm. Some prime contractors try to create the illusion that other team members are actually employees of their own consulting firm. To perpetuate this illusion, other team members are given business cards in the prime contractor's name and prohibited from passing out their own business cards when working on a project. I personally won't join teams where I have to play this game.

- Independent security consultants need to carefully consider the potential for a conflict of interest before joining a project team that also includes sellers of security products or services. While there is nothing strictly unethical about partnering with a guard company or security systems integrator, there can be challenges when you are called in to objectively evaluate these same companies on other projects in the future. To avoid the potential for these conflicts, I rarely enter into partnerships with sellers of security products or guard services.
- The teaming agreement should clearly specify who gets any follow-up work that is generated as a result of the initial project. For example, a security management consultant, technical security consultant, and cybersecurity consultant may team up to perform a security assessment for a client. The security management consultant acts as the prime consultant. After the assessment, the client decides that they need a consultant to design a new video surveillance system for the facility. Who gets this work? Does the client contract directly with the technical security consultant, or with the team that had the original contract?

Using Subcontractors

Independent security consultants who choose to work alone can still leverage their capabilities through the use of subcontractors. Subcontractors are independent entities that the consultant hires on a contract basis to perform certain project related tasks. Examples of work performed for security consultants by subcontractors include:

- Computer-aided drafting.
- Printing, collating, and binding of reports or publications.

- Professional photography or videos used for presentations or training materials.
- Research of public records and crime statistics and compilation of data for reports.
- Conducting photometric studies to determine lighting levels in parking lots.
- Professional editing of reports and other written materials.
- Creating as-built documentation of existing security systems by conducting field surveys of devices and cabling.

Please note that, unlike with teaming arrangements, the subcontractors listed above are only responsible for performing specific tasks, not completing entire portions of the consulting project. In general, subcontractors are used to perform specialized tasks that the consultant is not equipped to perform, or when a task can be performed more cost-effectively by the subcontractor.

Care should be taken when trying to use subcontractors to perform the core activities of your business. Many companies have attempted to get around employment taxes and other responsibilities imposed upon employers by declaring that their workers are "independent contractors" rather than employees. These are sometimes called "1099 workers" because of the federal tax form (Form 1099) that is sent to these workers at the end of each year.

For example, if you are a technical security consultant who designs security systems, and you use the services of another person to design security systems for you, that person may be considered by law to be an employee, not a subcontractor – regardless of what you choose to call them. Misclassifying an employee as a subcontractor can subject the employer to severe fines and penalties.

The Internal Revenue Service (IRS) has specific guidelines to help you to determine who is a subcontractor and who is an employee. Consultants contemplating the use of subcontractors should review these guidelines, and if questions remain, consult with their accounting advisor to get an opinion.

Hiring Employees

Some consultants choose to take their one-person security consulting practice to the next level by hiring employees. This usually happens after the individual consultant achieves a certain level of success working alone and begins to have to turn away work because they are simply too busy. Rather than turn this work away, the consultant hires first one and then another employee until at some point the consultant is now managing a multi-person consulting firm.

In the over thirty-five years that I have been in the security consulting business, I have seen cases of extreme success and extreme failure when consultants attempt to expand their business through the hiring of employees.

In my own personal case, I started off as a one-person consulting firm, and then gradually grew my business by hiring security system designers, security consultants, and CAD drafters. While adding employees allowed me to perform more work, I found that I was less happy and actually made less money during most of the years that I had employees.

What I ultimately discovered was this: being a successful independent security consultant and managing a successful multi-employee security consulting firm are two entirely different things. Just because you are good at one thing is no guarantee that you can be good at the other. I eventually decided that while I was a very good security consultant, my skills as a manager of people were probably mediocre at best.

More importantly, I found that I got my greatest joy from actually doing the consulting work itself, not from managing a group of other people. As my practice grew, I was delegating away more and more of the things that I loved to do, so that I could focus more and more on things that I didn't enjoy doing. This was not a recipe for personal satisfaction or happiness. I now operate as a sole practitioner once again and couldn't be happier.

Not everyone has had the same experience. I know of one man who started a security consulting and design practice which eventually grew to have multiple offices and more than 60 employees. This man was a genius when it came to marketing, and he loved the challenges associated with running a large consulting business. He was also a master at controlling costs, even gaining the reputation of being notoriously cheap, but always seemed to be able to turn a nice profit. His firm was eventually sold to a large public corporation for a multi-million-dollar sum.

I can currently think of at least a dozen other security consulting firms who operate with between five and twenty-five employees and appear to be successful.

Deciding to hire employees to grow your consulting business is a highly personal decision and one that should be made with great care. Here are a few things that you should consider when making this decision:

- Hiring another person to work for you is a tremendous responsibility. The livelihood of this person and their family is now in your hands. You are expected to make payroll every pay period without fail, regardless of how slow business has been or how long it takes clients to pay you.
- Payroll tax deposits and insurance premiums must be paid like clockwork. Taxes deducted from payroll checks must be deposited in a timely manner. Using these funds to pay other expenses is considered unforgiveable and is punished severely by the IRS and other regulatory agencies.
- The hiring of your first employee requires that your business register as an employer and sign-up to pay employment taxes of various types. Worker's compensation and other types of insurance may also be required. Having employees and making payroll greatly increases the complexity of your accounting system and the time associated with performing administrative tasks. There is an old joke that says when you hire your first employee, you need to hire a second one just to handle the additional administrative work. While this is somewhat of an exaggeration, it is not too far from the truth.

- Your own personal productivity as a consultant will go down as a result of hiring employees. The time it takes to recruit, train, and manage employees is non-billable. Interruptions by employees throughout the day can make you less effective as a consultant yourself. You must spend additional time on marketing and sales activities in order to keep everyone in the firm busy. You need to make sure that the benefits gained by hiring employees aren't completely offset by the loss in your own personal productivity.
- When you have multiple people on the payroll, you not only need enough work to keep them all busy, but you also need to make sure that the type of work is evenly balanced between disciplines. For example, if you have security consultants, security designers, and CAD drafters, you need to make sure that ample work is available in each category. I have never been more frustrated than when I had CAD drafters sitting idle while my security consultants were overloaded doing assessment projects.
- Hiring employees that have previous security industry experience but who have never worked as a consultant can require a substantial investment in training. I estimate that it can take from 6 to 18 months for a person with previous industry experience to become fully productive as a consultant.
- Employees must be closely supervised to see that they are producing work that is of an acceptable quality. Turning employees loose on projects without adequate supervision can quickly destroy a reputation that has taken you years to build.
- Always understand that even the best of employees will never care as much about your business or clients as you will. It is unrealistic to expect employees to make the same type of sacrifices for your business as you do.

- Employees are free to leave your business at any time and can take your proprietary business techniques and sometimes even your clients along with them. Although you can reduce your risks somewhat by having employees sign non-disclosure and non-compete agreements, I find that attempting to enforce these agreements is costly, creates ill-will, and is rarely worth the effort.
- You can invest hundreds of hours in developing and training employees only to have them leave you for other opportunities. One of the very best security designers I ever had was a person with no security industry experience who I trained from scratch. I thought that he would be with me forever. One day he came to me and told me that he was leaving to become a missionary in Africa. Not wanting to interfere with the plans of God, I wished him well and sent him on his way. He left, taking probably $50,000 worth of training along with him.

Joining a Larger Firm

If an independent security consultant has achieved any level of success, at some point they will likely be approached and asked to join a larger consulting firm. While these are sometimes portrayed as a "merger" or "acquisition", in most cases the independent consultant is actually asked to close their business and to join the larger company as an employee.

In some cases, the larger firm may offer a signing bonus or stock options in return for the independent consultant bringing in any clients and ongoing projects that they might have. The larger firm seldom actually purchases the consultant's business, typically due to concerns about potential liability.

The offer to join a larger firm can be tempting because it offers a steady paycheck and good health insurance and other benefits. There may also be an opportunity to work on larger projects for a more diverse range of clients. You also no longer need to worry about paying for your own business expenses and may be able to spend more time actually doing consulting work rather than selling and running a business.

However, I have found that once you have tasted the freedom of self-employment, it can be difficult to go back to work for someone else. The consulting techniques that you developed while you were on your own may be different than those at your new firm, requiring you to completely change the way that you operate.

When you're employed by another consulting firm, you have two masters to satisfy: your employer and your clients. At times, their interests may clash, putting you in a difficult position.

Some larger consulting firms have an "eat what you kill" compensation model where consultants are paid based on the revenue they create, the clients that they bring in, and the number of billable hours that they generate. This can create a highly competitive environment that is uncomfortable for some people who are used to a more laid-back atmosphere.

Like the decision to hire employees, closing your practice to join a larger firm is a highly personal decision and one that should be made with great care.

Chapter 15 - Continuing Education

Importance of Continuing Education

The security consultant's stock in trade are skills, experience, and knowledge. Unlike a retail merchant whose inventory sits on a shelf, the consultant's inventory consists of the knowledge and skills that are contained within the mind. I refer to this as the consultant's "intellectual inventory".

Just like with other types of inventory, some portion of the consultant's intellectual inventory becomes obsolete over time and needs to be replenished with new inventory. Independent security consultants who fail to update their intellectual inventory on a regular basis start to deliver outdated services to clients and soon become irrelevant.

To keep their intellectual inventory fresh, consultants need to continue to update their knowledge and skills throughout the life of their consulting career. This requires deliberate effort: there is rarely extra time in the busy consultant's schedule and the urge to complete billable projects will always seem to outweigh the need to refresh your skills. Resist this urge and make a conscious decision to set aside time to improve your expertise, even if it occasionally means turning away billable work.

Self-Study

One of the best forms of continuing education is self-study. Here are a few ways that independent security consultants can continue to educate themselves:

- Spend a half-hour per day reading security-related newsletters, blogs, and magazines. If possible, make this a part of your daily routine. I do my reading every morning when I am having my first cup of coffee.
- Read at least one new book per month on a topic directly related to your area of security specialty, or on a topic in a closely aligned field. This is a great way to make effective use of time when traveling by bus, train, or airplane.

- Subscribe to and actively participate in online forums related to your specialty.
- Make it a point to learn about one new type of technology related to your security consulting practice each month. This should include hardware devices, software, and cloud-based services. If possible, actually touch and use the technology yourself.

Conferences and Exhibitions

Independent security consultants should attend at least one professional conference each year. Depending on your area of specialty, this could be the GSX Annual Conference, ISC East or ISC West, the IAPSC Annual Conference, the Annual $(ISC)^2$ Security Congress, IAHSS Annual Conference & Exhibition, or any one of a number of other events.

Conferences are expensive when you factor in the costs of travel, lodging, and the loss of billable time. However, you should consider conferences to be a necessary part of your overhead costs and include an allowance for them in your annual budget.

Get the most out of conferences by attending the educational sessions that are offered. Spend time visiting the booths of the various manufacturers of security products and services. Network with fellow security consultants and others in the security industry that you may have worked with in the past.

Many organizations such as ASIS also hold regional conferences or seminars. While usually not as elaborate as the national conferences, these events can be less costly to attend and offer the added benefit of allowing you to network with local security professionals in your geographical area.

Webinars

Many professional organizations and equipment manufacturers offer educational webinars on a variety of security related topics. Webinars can be an effective way to keep on top of emerging trends in your area of practice and can be attended from the convenience of your home or office.

The Emotional Challenges Faced by Consultants

The new consultant can face a number of unexpected emotional challenges when the realities of running an independent security consulting practice become known. Some of these challenges include:

Where are My Friends Now?

Security consultants who previously held high-ranking positions in the corporate world or government often become accustomed to receiving a certain level of respect from colleagues, vendors, and other professional associates.

When they announce their intention to start their own consulting practice, they often receive encouraging comments from their colleagues who say things such as "*I know a lot of people who will hire you*", "*the market definitely needs a consultant with your expertise*", or "*I'm sure that our company will be able to give you a lot of work*".

Once they are finally out on their own, they often find that colleagues who previously stated their support are in actuality not able to provide much help. Calls that were quickly returned when the consultant had a large corporation behind them are sometimes not returned as quickly or at all when the consultant is on their own. Promises to make introductions and to provide business leads never become a reality. Peers from other large corporations who the consultant had previously thought of as friends now seem to act as strangers.

Many new consultants quickly become discouraged when these things happen and start to question their own self-worth. They didn't realize how much of their identity was predicated on employment at their previous job.

The reality is this: when you go out on your own, you cannot rely on friends and previous relationships to sustain you as a consultant. If in fact some of your past contacts are able to be of help, that's great. But just don't expect it or rely upon it to pay your bills.

Once you are on your own, you need to establish your own new identity as a consultant and develop the appropriate types of new relationships that can allow you to succeed.

Feeling of Isolation

Security consultants who previously worked for a large corporation or government agency were probably used to coming into contact with a large number of fellow employees each day. There were people to socialize with, people to bounce ideas off of, and people to go to lunch with. Whether the consultant realized it or not, the work routine and daily commute also exposed the consultant to new personalities, concepts, and visual impressions that provided stimulus to the mind.

When a consultant goes out on their own, they will often be working out of a home office and can have no contact with anyone outside of their family for days or even weeks on end. This can often result in depression and a feeling of isolation. Some people also find that they have trouble coming up with new ideas or thinking clearly. To combat these symptoms, the following is recommended:

- Develop an informal relationship with other independent security consultants and communicate with them frequently. Even a five-minute phone conversation with someone who is in a situation similar to your own can work wonders.
- Try to get out of your home office at least once per day, even if it is just for a quick trip to the store or post office.
- Meet at least once or twice weekly for coffee with an influencer or past client.
- Once or twice per week, take your laptop computer and work at a coffee shop or library. Many of my very best reports were written at a Starbucks.

Avoiding Emotional Highs and Lows

Most new security consultants become overly optimistic when they start to receive new business inquiries and start to write their first proposals. They are certain that they will receive the project and begin to celebrate and brag of their accomplishment to their family and friends, even though a firm commitment from the client was never made. When the project falls through, the consultant is deeply disappointed and depressed, and ashamed to tell their family and friends of the bad news.

While a sense of optimism is healthy, consultants should never consider a project won until a signed agreement is in hand. When a new sales opportunity presents itself, be grateful, but remember, it is an opportunity – not a guarantee of work. You will win some opportunities and lose others, so try not to get too excited either way. You can tell family and friends about opportunities, but don't overstate your chances of success. Getting too attached to any one sales opportunity can be emotionally destructive.

Do the best you can with every sales opportunity or proposal, and then move on to the next one and do the same. Success in selling is a numbers game, and if you do your job correctly, you will win more than your fair share of jobs. When you do lose a job, consider it to be a learning experience. Try to learn the reason why you lost the business and identify ways in which you can make your future proposals better. Stay positive. Don't dwell on your failures or blame the client or your competitors.

Dealing with Messy Situations

Many new consultants are surprised at just how disorganized their potential clients seem to be. The RFP that the client issued is poorly written and confusing. When talking with client representatives, they don't seem to know what they want and give you conflicting information. When you are finally awarded the contract, the client is unable to provide you with all of the materials that you need to get started. When attending client meetings, people don't show up on time and are unprepared.

You ask yourself: "Why is this client so screwed up? I could do my job a lot better if this client wasn't so disorganized. Why can't I seem to get any good clients?"

The truth is, the majority of clients seeking your services probably will have weaknesses in all areas of their organization, not just in security. The same management style that caused the issues that created the need for your services probably has created problems in other areas of their business.

Security consultants who don't want to deal with disorganized clients are like physicians who don't want to treat sick patients. Often times, the security consultant's role is as much to provide needed organizational skills as it is to provide security expertise. Poorly written RFPs are often a cry for help, and disorganized and confused clients are exactly the type of people most in need of your services.

Learn to deal with the frustration of working with disorganized clients. See messy situations as opportunities to apply both your professional organizational skills and your security skills. Develop a reputation as a consultant that can solve tough problems and who stays calm in a sea of chaos.

Rejection of Recommendations

Beginning consultants often get their feelings hurt or feel depressed when they discover that a client has not implemented a single recommendation from the report that they so painstakingly crafted.

As an independent security consultant, you will often make recommendations that clients may not implement. In fact, the client that implements all or even most of what the consultant has recommended is usually the exception, not the rule.

Clients reject recommendations for a variety of reasons: they may not have the money available to implement them, they don't feel that the recommended actions would be well received by their stakeholders, or simply feel that what is being recommended is "overkill" for their particular needs, no matter how good a case the consultant has made for it in their report.

At times, the consultant may have been hired simply because it was a suggestion from someone in upper management. The employees at the operating level have their own ideas about security and had little or no intention of ever implementing anything that the consultant recommended.

Consultants should try not to take rejections of their recommendations personally. They should always thoroughly evaluate the client's needs and offer them their best professional advice. Your job is to present options to the client – what they choose to do with them is out of your control. Ultimately, the client must make their own decisions and accept responsibility for their own actions or inactions.

Project Attachment

As an independent security consultant, you will sometimes work on a project for weeks, months, or even years. You develop a deep attachment to the project and to the client representatives that you are working with.

Suddenly, you are told that the project is cancelled or that your services are no longer needed. You lose all touch with the people you were working with and no longer have any idea of what is going on with the project.

Many consultants feel a deep emotional attachment to a project and suffer a great sense of loss when it is suddenly gone. This was their "baby" that they carefully nurtured and now someone has snatched it away. Unfortunately, this type of thing happens all the time in the consulting world: you are a "hired gun" that serves at the client's pleasure and the client has no obligation to you beyond paying you your fee.

New consultants should understand this from the start and try not to develop too deep of a personal attachment to any one client or project.

Slumps

As your consulting practice grows, you may sometimes lose your confidence, have doubt about the path that you have chosen, or feel like you are stuck in a rut. This can be the result of too many rejections in a row, burnout, boredom, the lack of clearly defined goals, or personal issues.

Slumps such as these are experienced by nearly every consultant at one time or another. To work your way out of a slump, the following is suggested:

- Identify what may be causing the slump.
- Change your daily routine by switching up your schedule or performing tasks in a different order.
- Work in a place other than your home or office for a day or two.
- Reflect on your past successes, problems solved, and times when your services greatly benefited a client.
- Divide complex projects up into small manageable tasks and begin to complete some of the less complicated ones first. Making progress on a few easy things can give you a sense of progress and help to propel you forward.
- Take care of yourself: get plenty of sleep, exercise, and eat right.
- Regularly stop to take breaks. Sometimes something as simple as a walk around the block can clear your head and put you back on track.
- Reach out to a trusted friend or professional colleague to discuss your situation and seek guidance. Often just talking about a problem is helpful.

Walking the Ethical Tightrope

As an independent security consultant, you will become privy to a large amount of sensitive and confidential information. When working for clients, you will learn much information that could be extremely detrimental to the client if improperly disclosed.

When reviewing vendor RFPs and contracts, you will learn much proprietary information about specific providers of security products and guard services, including their pricing structure, overhead costs, and strategic marketing plans. You will probably also have access to their client lists and information concerning their key personnel. When helping a client to prepare a specification or RFP for a guard contract or security system upgrade, you probably have lots of information that if improperly disclosed, could provide an advantage to one of the bidders.

Almost all people entering the consulting profession would say that they know how to keep secrets and wouldn't improperly release any type of sensitive information. Although they have good intentions, they probably don't realize just how hard it is to keep from inadvertently disclosing sensitive information as they go about their daily activities.

Most security consultants come from previous careers in security and law enforcement and probably know hundreds of people in the security industry. Many of these people may have become close friends. The potential to inadvertently disclose sensitive information is a constant danger, particularly in social settings when one is relaxed and has their guard down.

As part of their daily activities, security consultants reach out to suppliers of security products and services, often seeking advice. As a part of the conversation, it is natural to want to give specific information about the projects they are working on. When asking a supplier for a favor, it is natural to want to offer something in return. This can result in situations where sensitive information is inadvertently disclosed as a part of a conversation.

Finally, there is our ego. When working for prestigious clients and on high-profile projects, it is natural to want to brag about them, sometimes sharing details that should have been kept a secret with friends and business associates.

The new security consultant needs to remain especially vigilant when it comes to keeping sensitive information confidential. If this is done correctly, friends who you once freely shared information with may start to make comments about how secretive you have become. Consider this to be a compliment and explain the reasons why you cannot discuss certain matters.

Common Mistakes

The following are some common mistakes made by new security consultants as they go about conducting their daily consulting activities:

- Thinking that you have nothing more to learn in order to be a consultant.
- Being afraid to ask more experienced consultants and other professionals for help.
- Thinking you can be your own accountant or lawyer.
- Presuming that you know in advance what a potential client wants or needs.
- Starting a security consulting practice without adequate financing to sustain yourself through the early years.
- Overestimating the value of your previous job title or position.
- Not having or not following a business plan.
- Ignoring competition from suppliers of security products and services who also provide "security consulting".
- Forgetting that the benefits of using an independent security consultant must be sold before you can sell yourself.
- Trying to be all things to all people.
- Reducing your consulting fees to an unprofitable level just so that you can get work.
- Making business decisions based on ego rather than common sense.

- Establishing your monthly overhead based on your best month rather than your worst month.
- Becoming overly reliant on obtaining business from only a single client.
- Not having a proactive sales and marketing program in place.
- Relying on social media as your only method of marketing.
- Stopping your sales and marketing activities when you begin to start getting busy.
- Being so busy with projects that you neglect to run your business.
- Taking on more work than you can handle.
- Agreeing to unrealistic project completion schedules.
- Taking on projects that you are not qualified to perform.
- Not staying in touch with past clients.
- Starting work on projects without a written agreement.
- Entering into relationships that compromise your independence.
- Spending time networking with people you like but who have no ability to buy or even recommend your services.
- Continuously trying to sell a service that the marketplace has said it is unwilling to buy.
- Not working as hard for yourself as you did for others.
- Quitting too soon.

Chapter 17 - Becoming a Superstar Consultant

Not all independent security consultants have the same goals.

Some people starting a consulting practice have retired from a successful career in the military, law enforcement, or private security and only want to do security consulting part-time. These people really don't need the money and are doing consulting because they enjoy doing it and because it gives them something to occupy their time. Although not recommended, these people can probably ignore most of the advice in this book and still achieve their goals.

Other people are starting a security consulting practice as an alternative to being employed at a full-time job. These people are still in their peak earning years and need a steady income to support their family and set aside money for retirement. These people must take their security consulting practice seriously and should carefully follow the advice given in this book to achieve their goals.

Finally, there are people who are extremely ambitious and want to operate their security consulting practice at the highest possible level. I call these people "superstar consultants" and they represent probably 10% or less of all independent security consultants. Superstar consultants can earn two or three times the money of other consultants and enjoy a reputation as being "one of the best of the best" in the profession.

In addition to following the advice given elsewhere in this book, superstar consultants need to cultivate the habits of top performers in other fields. Becoming a superstar consultant requires hard work and making some sacrifices in your personal life.

The following are some tips for becoming a superstar consultant based on observing other top performing security consultants over the last 35 years. Even if you choose not to make the sacrifices necessary to operate at the superstar level, some or all of these tips may be beneficial to you.

Follow a Structured Daily Routine

Being self-employed is a two-edged sword. You have complete freedom to set your own schedule and to do as you please, but if you are not disciplined, you may find that you are accomplishing little or nothing in the course of a day.

Unless they have a specific project or appointment scheduled, too many consultants have no real plan for their day. They get up late, spend the morning reading the news and social media postings, and then respond to a few emails. They start work on an article they are writing for a newsletter and find they need to do some research on a specific topic. They watch a YouTube video on the topic but get distracted and end up watching several other videos unrelated to their work.

Soon, it is time for lunch. After lunch, they check their emails and social media again and then get back to work on their article. They get interrupted by a call from a buddy and spend an hour on the phone. They work on their article a little more and soon it is time for dinner. A whole day has gone by, and they have done almost nothing to achieve their business goals. If they had operated this way when they worked for their previous employer, they probably would have been fired.

You need to treat your consulting practice as a real job and establish a structured work routine. You should consistently put in at least a full eight-hour day, five days per week. A daily schedule should be created where you set aside specific blocks of time for specific business activities. During these blocks of time, you need to work exclusively on the activity you have designated for that time period without interruption.

When first establishing a practice, the consultant should spend the majority of their time on marketing and business development. An example of what a daily schedule during this early stage of the practice might look like is provided below.

7:00A – 8:00A	Identify prospective clients and enter into marketing database
8:00A – 10:00A	Make phone calls, and send emails and direct mail letters to prospective clients
10:00A -11:00	Write new client proposals and follow-up on previously submitted proposals
11:00A – 12:00P	Make calls and send emails to influencers and competitors
12:00P – 1:00P	Lunch
1:00P – 3:00P	Attend in-person or teleconference sales appointments with potential clients
3:00P – 4:00P	Scan public procurement websites to identify potential RFP/RFP opportunities
4:00P – 5:00P	Create and publish content on website, blog, or in online forums
5:00P – 5:30P	Prepare work plan for following day

Daily Schedule for New Consultant

As you begin to take on projects, your daily schedule will change. You will need to spend more of your time on project work, but you should always dedicate at least some time each week to sales and marketing. You will also need to add dedicated time for administrative activities such as billing and accounting. An example of what a daily schedule of an established consultant might look like is provided below.

7:00A – 7:30A	Identify prospective clients and enter into marketing database
7:30A – 8:00A	Make phone calls, and send emails and direct mail letters to prospective clients and past clients
8:00A -9:00A	Write new client proposals and follow-up on previously submitted proposals
10:00A – 12:00P	Work on billable client project
12:00P – 1:00P	Lunch with influencer
1:00P – 4:00P	Work on billable client project
4:00P – 5:00P	Send invoices, pay bills, enter data in accounting system
5:00P – 6:00P	Create and publish content on website, blog, or in online forums
6:00P – 6:30P	Prepare work plan for following day

Daily Schedule for Established Consultant

The schedule of an established consultant will likely vary from day to day, with some days dedicated entirely to project work, other days dedicated to sales, marketing, and administrative work, and some days that include a combination of both. The important thing is to establish a balanced schedule throughout the week so that no area of your consulting practice is neglected.

Once you develop your schedule, you should attempt to stick to it as rigidly as possible. While some interruptions are unavoidable, you should work each day according to a plan rather than responding to the random set of circumstances that happen to come your way.

There is an old saying that goes "*plan your work and work your plan*". Although this has become a cliché, I have found this advice to be essential if you wish to operate at the superstar level.

Treat Time as If It Were Currency and Spend It Wisely

Everyone has the same number of minutes each day. Time is an irreplaceable commodity – once it is gone you can never get it back. When planning and executing your daily schedule, be sure that you are maximizing the value of every minute.

Many of us have had occasions when we were getting ready for a vacation or other trip and had a multitude of things that had to be done on the day before we left. Somehow, we managed to get more things done in a single day than we would normally accomplish in a week. This illustrates that we all have the capacity to do much more each day if we simply put our mind to it.

Take Control of Your Day

Don't let incoming phone calls, emails, and social media posts control your day. Superstar consultants understand the importance of taking control of their time rather than reacting to constant interruptions throughout the day.

Constantly checking your email and social media throughout the day is a bad habit. Dedicate specific blocks of your time in your schedule to respond to emails and social media posts and avoid the temptation of doing it at other times.

Along the same lines, unless you are expecting an urgent business or personal call, let your calls go to voice mail and return them during the block of time that you have specifically set aside for that purpose.

It can take a while to change old habits, but once you do, you will see a remarkable increase in your productivity.

Know Your Peak Performance Hours

Every one of us has specific times during the day when we do our best work. During these times, we think better, are more creative, and have a greater sense of purpose. I call these "peak performance hours".

Different people have different peak performance hours. I had a friend and mentor who did his best work between midnight and 4:00 AM (much to the displeasure of his wife). Another associate of mine finds that her peak performance hours are in the early afternoon between 1:00 PM and 4:00 PM. Some people may have two peak performance periods, perhaps one in the morning and then another one in the early evening.

Those who want to operate at the superstar level need to identify their peak performance hours and try to schedule their most important work during these periods. Less important work should be scheduled outside of these hours.

My peak performance hours are the first three hours of the day, usually between about 6:00 AM and 9:00 AM. I try to do most of my writing and other creative work during these hours. I do my best to avoid squandering these precious hours doing routine work that doesn't require much thought. I schedule these more mundane tasks for later in the day when my mind is not working at its best.

Push Past Your Comfort Zone

When asked, most successful independent security consultants will say that they love what they do and couldn't imagine doing anything else. This is not 100% accurate – most consultants have some aspects of their work that they dislike or sometimes even hate.

For example, many consultants dislike some or all the sales activities necessary to get new clients, specially making "cold calls" to prospects. Other consultants hate doing paperwork and may be months behind in their billing and tax returns. Still others dislike confrontations and have a hard time delivering the bad news that a consultant sometimes must deliver.

Achieving success is not always convenient and requires you to sometimes do things that you don't want to do. In fact, one way to prioritize your to-do list is to look at all the tasks on the list and then pick the task that you would least like to do. Chances are, this is probably the most important item on the list and the one that will provide the most reward when completed.

Those who want to operate at a superstar level must do things that they may not like to do and stretch themselves by actively seeking out and performing activities that may be outside of their comfort zone.

Surround Yourself with the Right People

The behaviors, attitudes, and beliefs of the people around you can have a great influence on you over time. Superstar consultants surround themselves with other successful people, not only other security consultants, but professionals in other related fields. They actively seek out people who are already achieving the level of success that they wish to achieve. They expand their knowledge by associating with people that are more intelligent than they are and don't feel that they have to compete with them.

Superstar consultants are coachable and actively seek advice from others in the security consulting profession. They ask others to critique their work and are willing to listen to constructive criticism – even if it is painful to hear.

Superstar consultants thrive on positivity and associate with people who are optimistic and encouraging. They avoid associating with people who have negative attitudes, are always complaining, and feel that the world is mistreating them.

Develop a Bias for Action

Superstar consultants know that procrastination can prevent them from achieving their goals and develop a habit of acting quickly and decisively. They know that taking any type of action, even if imperfect, is better than doing nothing at all.

Stay Laser Focused on Your Specialty

Superstar consultants know what they are best at and try to concentrate exclusively on projects where their specialized expertise provides the most value to the client. They avoid taking on projects that are outside of their specialty and refer them to other consultants when appropriate.

Establish a Reputation as An Expert

Superstar consultants strive to become a recognized expert in their specialty. They achieve this by writing books and magazine articles, serving as volunteer leaders of professional organizations, speaking at industry events, and making themselves available for interviews by the news media.

Know Your Worth

Superstar consultants know their value and charge appropriately for their services. They are never the "low-cost provider" in their specialty and often charge substantially more than their competitors. They stand their ground on fees with their clients and insist on being treated fairly and with respect.

Work Longer Hours

Superstar consultants know that you can't achieve extraordinary results by doing ordinary things. They are willing to put in the extra hours necessary to achieve the level of success that they desire, knowing that this may require some sacrifices in their personal life.

Many consultants operating at the superstar level extend the length of their workday by starting work one hour earlier in the morning and working one hour longer in the afternoon. This increases their productivity potential by 25% and adds the equivalent of sixty additional working days to their year.

Act as If You are Starting from Zero Each Day

Superstar consultants take nothing for granted and act as if they are starting from nothing each day. They know that no matter how well-established that their business is, market conditions can change rapidly, causing a large backlog of work to suddenly evaporate. Even when they are already very successful, they stay attuned to the marketplace and aggressively pursue new clients and new opportunities.

Stay in Touch with Your Clients

Superstar consultants know that existing clients are a precious resource. They check-in with past clients several times per year to see how they are doing, regardless of whether they think the client has a current need for additional services or not.

Keep Your Commitments

Sadly, in today's business world, a surprising number of people fail to keep their commitments and offer excuses such as "*I'm sorry, I had an emergency come up, so I wasn't able to finish your report*", or "*sorry, I'm late, traffic on the freeway was a mess*", or " *I didn't get your email – it must have been sent to my spam folder*", or " *a lot of unexpected things came up, so our fees for this project will be substantially higher than I quoted you*", or a myriad of other excuses.

While in some cases these excuses may be true, the fact is that excuses, even if they seem justified, do not change the fact that something wasn't done as promised or expected.

I have also found that it is usually always the same people who seem to be making excuses over and over, while other people seem to always keep their commitments 100% of the time.

Superstar consultants strive to fall into the latter group and always try to do exactly what they said they were going to do, exactly when they said they were going to do it. This may sometimes require working through the night and weekend to complete a project, arriving much earlier than needed to be sure that they are on time, and occasionally doing a project at a loss. By doing this, they establish a reputation for always keeping their word and place themselves in that rare group of professionals that clients can always rely upon.

Deliver More Than Expected

Superstar consultants always go the extra mile and deliver just a little bit more than expected for their clients. Here are just a few examples:

- A security consultant performing an assessment might recommend the creation of a security policies and procedures manual. As a bonus, the consultant might include an editable template that could be used by the client to create the policies and procedures manual themselves if they chose not to hire the consultant to do it.
- A security consultant completing a security design project for a client might provide a written document at no charge that has recommendations for preventive maintenance and spare parts for the newly installed systems.
- A security consultant may have been required to create floor plan drawings of a client's building from scratch because no existing drawings were available. As a bonus, the consultant might provide blank copies of these drawings in editable format to the client so that they can be used for other purposes (planning of furniture layouts, location of inventory, etc.)

The goal is to let the client know that you truly care about them and make them feel that they have received more than they paid for.

Continually Review Your Performance

Superstar consultants are never fully satisfied with their performance and are always looking for ways to get better. They never get complacent and are continually working to sharpen their skills.

At the completion of every project, they always take the time to conduct an "after-action" review to identify things that went right, things that went wrong, and lessons learned.

Similarly, they review the outcome of every sales proposal, whether successful or not, to try to determine why they won or lost the business and what they can do better in future proposals.

Closing Remarks

I appreciate you taking the time to read this book and hope that some of the information provided is helpful to you as you start your independent security consulting practice.

I encourage you to consider me to be a resource to you as you begin your journey. Please don't hesitate to call or email if you have a question or need help with a topic that I have not covered in this book. If I can't help you directly, I will try to point you in the right direction. Also, please feel free to connect with me on LinkedIn and follow me on X (formerly Twitter).

Finally, whether you found this book to be helpful or not, I would greatly appreciate it if you could take a few moments to leave an honest review on Amazon or other site where you purchased it. Your feedback not only helps me as the author but also helps other readers to decide if the book is right for them.

I sincerely wish you the greatest of success in your consulting practice.

Michael A. Silva, CPP, CSC
PO Box 8799
Covington, WA 98042
Telephone: (888) 645-2299
Email: mikes@silvaconsultants.com
Website: www.silvaconsultants.com
X (Twitter): @silvaconsultant
Linked-In: www.linkedin.com/in/silvaconsultants

About the Author

Michael A. Silva is an independent security consultant located in the Seattle, Washington area. Michael has over 50 years of security industry experience, including over 38 years as a consultant. Michael started in the security industry at the age of 14, when he began installing burglar alarm systems. Michael has had a life-long interest in security, electronics, radios, and business.

Over the past 38 years, Michael has successfully completed consulting and design projects for a wide variety of different types of facilities, including corporate headquarters facilities, data centers, manufacturing facilities, warehouses and distribution centers, hospitals and healthcare facilities, biotechnology and pharmaceutical facilities, educational facilities, government facilities, public utilities, multifamily housing complexes, and the residences of corporate executives and other high net worth individuals.

In addition to practicing as a security consultant, Michael frequently serves as a mentor to people who wish to enter the security consulting profession themselves.

Michael is board-certified as a Certified Protection Professional (CPP) by ASIS International and as a Certified Security Consultant (CSC) by the International Association of Professional Security Consultants (IAPSC)

Michael is the author of two other books: "*Protecting Apartments, Condominiums, and Gated Communities: A Guide to Security for Homeowner's Associations and Property Managers*", and "*The Security Consultant's Guide to Home Security: 101 Tips to Make Your Home Safer and More Secure*".

www.ingramcontent.com/pod-product-compliance
Lightning Source LLC
Chambersburg PA
CBHW060358220326
41598CB00023B/2953